P9-CFX-450

MEDIAEVAL SOURCES
IN TRANSLATION

18

THE LIFE
OF
COLA DI RIENZO

Translated with an Introduction

by

JOHN WRIGHT

PONTIFICAL INSTITUTE OF MEDIAEVAL STUDIES

For Jennifer
romanina

LIBRARY OF CONGRESS CATALOGUING DATA

Vita di Cola di Rienzo. English.
  The life of Cola di Rienzo / translated with an introd. by John
Wright. – Toronto: Pontifical Institute of Mediaeval Studies, 1975.
  166 p.; 21 cm.
  (Mediaeval sources in translation, ISSN 0316-0874; 18)
  Translation of La vita di Cola di Rienzo, edited by A. M.
Ghisalberti.
  Bibliography p. [155]-157.
  Includes index.
  ISBN 0-88844-267-X.

  1. Rienzo, Cola di, d. 1354.   2. Rome (City)—History—476-
1420.   I. Ghisalberti, Alberto Maria.   II. Wright, John.
II. Pontifical Institute of Mediaeval Studies.   III. Title.
IV. Series.

DG811.6.V6513   1975   945'.632'050924   76-362559

© 1975 by
Pontifical Institute of Mediaeval Studies
59 Queen's Park Crescent East
Toronto, Ontario, Canada M5S 2C4

PRINTED BY HIGNELL PRINTING, WINNIPEG, MANITOBA

CONTENTS

Acknowledgments 12

INTRODUCTION 13
    Cola di Rienzo 15
    The *Life of Cola di Rienzo* 20
    Note on the translation 28

BOOK ONE

The Life of Cola de Rienzi, Roman, Valorous Captain,
with all the Valiant Deeds he did against the Powerful
Barons of Rome, and of the Journey he made
to Pope Clement in Avignon.
Read, read, that I may make you lift your eyebrows
at his prowess.

Chapter One. — Parents, birth, character, and profession of Cola
di Rienzo; origin of his ideas; his embassy to Pope Clement
in Avignon and his return 31
Chapter Two. — In an assembly Cola makes a speech sharply
criticizing the officials and rulers of the people of Rome; for
this he is struck on the cheek by Andreozzo Colonna. He
also admonishes the people with a mysterious picture   32
Chapter Three. — At another time in St. John Lateran he admonishes the people with a speech describing the authority
formerly granted by the Roman people to the Emperor Vespasian, and also with mysterious figures 35
Chapter Four. — The barons of Rome mock Cola. With a picture
at Sant' Angelo in Pescheria, and in other ways, he predicts
his ascendancy, and holds a meeting for the reform of the
state 37
Chapter Five. — Description of the condition of Rome in those
times. Cola reveals himself as chief of the reform of the
government of Rome. He comes armed to the Campidoglio
and addresses the people 40

Chapter Six. — On the Campidoglio Cola publishes the laws for implementing the good government of Rome. On account of this the people proclaim him lord with absolute power, and he remains on the Campidoglio with the Pope's vicar   41

Chapter Seven. — Stefano della Colonna returns to Rome, angry at Cola because of these events, and threatens him. He is, however, ordered to leave Rome, as are all the barons; this they do. And Cola has himself confirmed by the people, and obtains for himself and the Pope's vicar the titles of Tribunes and liberators of the people   43

Chapter Eight. — The barons conspire against Cola, but can reach no agreement. They are, however, summoned and forced by him to swear to support the good government of Rome; the judges and notaries do likewise   44

Chapter Nine. — Cola establishes the House of Justice and Peace for the reconciliation of disputes, and administers justice so diligently that every evildoer flees in terror. In these times a monster is born in Rome   46

Chapter Ten. — The Tribune sends letters to the Pope and all the princes of Europe concerning his ascendancy and government   47

Chapter Eleven. — The Tribune hangs Martino di Porto, a tyrannical aristocrat, to frighten the others   48

Chapter Twelve. — Because of the rigorous justice of the Tribune the aristocrats of Rome become so terrified that no further injustices occur, and even the Sultan of Babylon is frightened of him   50

Chapter Thirteen. — How the Tribune led his procession through the city, and how he was received by the clergy of St. Peter's when he visited that church   51

Chapter Fourteen. — The Tribune continues to exercise his justice, punishing criminals; he builds a palisade around the Palace of the Campidoglio, using all the fortifications of the barons of Rome, and forcing them and the former Senators to contribute to the repair of the Palace of the Campidoglio   53

Chapter Fifteen. — The Tribune organizes a militia of infantrymen and cavalrymen, and afterwards summons the aristo-

crats to render obedience and pay the hearth tax. All obey
except Janni di Vico, Tyrant of Viterbo, who however is deprived of his office by Cola   54
Chapter Sixteen. — The Tribune decides to go to war against
Janni di Vico; he names Cola Orsino his captain, who
besieges and captures the city of Vetralla. But Janni, hearing
that the Tribune is planning to come in person, submits, and
surrenders the Fortress of Rispampani, and is reinstated in
his Prefecture   55
Chapter Seventeen. — How the Tribune had foreseen all this in a
dream   57
Chapter Eighteen. — A discussion about dreams, which sometimes turn out true, like those of Fra Merulus, the Emperor
Marcian, and Cassius   58
Chapter Nineteen. — On the opinion of Aristotle concerning the
causes and variety of dreams   60
Chapter Twenty. — Many castles and fortresses are surrendered
to the Tribune, and many aristocrats submit to him. He
builds a chapel in his palace. Here he attends Mass, and his
wife is courted by the noblewomen, and his relatives by the
citizens   62
Chapter Twenty-One. — From far-off cities and castles people
come to Rome for justice which produces the best of effects.
And Cola, wishing to be sole lord, dismisses the Pope's
vicar and sends an embassy to His Holiness   63
Chapter Twenty-Two. — The principal cities and princes of
Christendom send ambassadors to the Tribune   64
Chapter Twenty-Three. — Concerning the magnificent responses
which Cola gave to the ambassadors   66
Chapter Twenty-Four. — Notable examples of the good justice of
the Tribune   68
Chapter Twenty-Five. — The Tribune takes the Order of Knighthood with great pomp and ceremony   69
Chapter Twenty-Six. — The Tribune, having been made a
knight, publicly summons the Pope, the College of Cardinals, the Bavarian, and the Imperial Electors, and performs other acts of jurisdiction   72

Chapter Twenty-Seven. — After the ceremony of knighthood the Tribune holds a solemn banquet, and then returns to the Campidoglio 73

Chapter Twenty-Eight. — The Tribune under various pretexts has the barons come to him, and then imprisons them 74

Chapter Twenty-Nine. — The Tribune has the death sentence announced to the imprisoned barons, but, allowing himself to be persuaded by the advice of some citizens, he frees them, giving them titles and gifts 76

Chapter Thirty. — The liberated barons plot against Cola, fortifying Marino and other strongholds, whence they are summoned by the Tribune. But instead of obeying they make forays as far as the gates of Rome 77

Chapter Thirty-One. — The Tribune goes to Marino with an army, captures the Castelluza, and does much damage; summoned again and again from there by the Pope's Legate, he returns to Rome 78

Chapter Thirty-Two. — The Colonna take up arms in Palestrina and march against Rome, with many other barons. The Tribune takes up arms, and, suspicious of the Prefect, who had come to help him, he puts him in prison 80

Chapter Thirty-Three. — The Colonna arrive at Rome with their army and find the gates barred. But while the army is passing in procession the gate is opened; Janni Colonna nobly enters there alone, where he is killed 82

Chapter Thirty-Four. — Stefano della Colonna and many other barons are killed, and the barons' army is routed 85

Chapter Thirty-Five. — The Tribune returns in triumph and lays down his crown and scepter in the Aracoeli. He allows no honor to be paid to the corpses of the three Colonna 87

Chapter Thirty-Six. — The Tribune is rebuked because he, like Hannibal, did not know how to use this victory 88

Chapter Thirty-Seven. — The Tribune makes his son Lorenzo Knight of the Victory; he begins to be proud and tyrannical, and frees the Prefect. Jordano da Marini harries Rome and many disorders arise 90

Chapter Thirty-Eight. — The Count Messer Janni Pipino, who was living in Rome at that time, stirs up the people, and

Cola and his wife flee Rome. He wanders from one place to another, and in Rome is painted as a traitor and condemned as a heretic by the Pope's Legate 92

Book Two

On the Semicentennial Jubilee in Rome

Chapter One. — Arrival in Rome of the Cardinal of Ceccano, Apostolic Legate, to start the Jubilee 97

Chapter Two. — Actions and authority of the Legate, and how, having been wounded by a javelin, he excommunicates the Tribune, whom he judges to be the author of treason 99

Chapter Three. — Death of the Cardinal Legate and description of the fate of his nephews 101

Book Three

How the Senator was stoned to Death by the Romans, and of the Magnificent Deeds done by Messer Egidio Conchese of Spain, Cardinal Legate, to recover the Patrimony, the March of Ancona, and Romagna

Chapter One. — The Senator of Rome is stoned to death by the people for having starved the city 107

Chapter Two. — Cardinal Egidio Conchese of Spain, sent into Italy by Pope Innocent as his Legate, forces Janni di Vico to restore Viterbo, Marta, and Canino, which he had usurped, to the Church 109

Chapter Three. — The Legate, having recovered Narni and Amelia, moves against the Malatesti in the March, where Galeotto Malatesta surrenders to him 111

Chapter Four. — Malatesta, in order to recover his brother, peacefully restores to the Legate the Church property he had seized. The cruel and tyrannical actions of Francesco Ordelaffi of Forli are recounted 113

Chapter Five. — The Legate, after having taken up arms against Ordelaffi, is recalled by the Pope, who sends the Abbot of Burgundy as new Legate 115

Chapter Six. — Cesena is taken by the Legate through the work
of four citizens 116

Chapter Seven. — Capture of the citadel of Cesena and imprisonment of Madonna Cia, wife of Ordelaffi 118

Chapter Eight. — The Legate repeatedly declares a crusade
against Ordelaffi, and finally strips him of Faenza and Bertinoro 119

BOOK FOUR

Second Part of the Life of Messer Nicola de Rienzi,
in which is contained his Return to Rome and Reassumption
of Power and the Deeds done by him after his Return,
and the Death dealt to him by the People of Rome

Chapter One. — Cola, after hiding for seven years in various
ways, goes to the Emperor, by whom he is most graciously
received 125

Chapter Two. — Cola goes to defend himself in Avignon; there
he is imprisoned and later absolved from the sentence of the
Cardinal of Ceccano 127

Chapter Three. — Cola returns to Rome with the Apostolic
Legate, where he receives many requests from the Roman
people 128

Chapter Four. — Cola, thanks to the aid of Messer Arimbaldo
and Messer Brettone, is prepared to try his luck again   130

Chapter Five. — Cola, made Senator of Rome by the Legate, sets
out for the city with the army he has hired 132

Chapter Six. — Public and solemn entrance of Cola into the city
of Rome 134

Chapter Seven. — Appearance and habits of Cola, who, after his
arrival in Rome, demands the obedience of the barons. His
orders are ignored and his messengers mistreated by Stefanello Colonna 135

Chapter Eight. — Cola, provoked by the disdain and the incursions of the Colonna, marches out against them and
exhorts his forces to battle with a beautiful speech   .. 137

Chapter Nine. — Cola, strengthened with auxiliary forces, besieges Palestrina 139

CONTENTS 11

Chapter Ten. — The siege of Palestrina is lifted, and Cola, suspecting that Messer Morreale wishes to betray him, has him imprisoned 140

Chapter Eleven. — Rigorous judgment and death of Messer Morreale 142

Chapter Twelve. — Cola announces his reasons for condemning Messer Morreale; he names Riccardo degli Anniballi, Lord of Monte Compatri, Captain of the People, and again besieges Palestrina and the Colonna 145

Chapter Thirteen. — Account of the unfortunate death of Cola 146

Select Bibliography 155

Index 159

ACKNOWLEDGMENTS

I owe a great debt of gratitude to the American Academy in Rome, where I was a Fellow from 1966 to 1968, where I was first introduced to Cola di Rienzo, and where I began my translation of the *Life* ; to the National Endowment for the Humanities, for a Younger Humanist Fellowship which enabled me, during my spare time, to complete some final revisions and corrections on the notes and text of the *Life* ; to Professor Marvin Becker, who freely offered me extensive bibliographical advice and made useful suggestions for improving the Introduction ; to several anonymous readers, especially the assessors of the Pontifical Institute of Mediaeval Studies, whose careful work saved me from making a number of errors; to Annamaria Cavicchia, *romana di Roma*, whose knowledge of her native dialect helped me in two important places where professional sources were of no avail ; and to my wife, who read my entire manuscript with patience and discernment and recommended several approaches for use in the introductory material which would not otherwise have occurred to me. I have tried to indicate the extent of my obligation to earlier scholars who have published material on Cola and the *Life* in my notes and bibliography.

Rome
16 June 1974

INTRODUCTION

Cola di Rienzo, the revolutionary leader of mediaeval Rome, has caught the imagination of historians and poets for hundreds of years. But of all the various attempts to recount his life and explain his character, from the time of Petrarch down to the present day, the most vivid and compelling portrait of this extraordinary figure still remains the anonymous contemporary biography known as the *Life of Cola di Rienzo*. Since the author of the *Life*, with an insouciance which an outsider might claim to be typically Roman, makes no attempt to explain the historical, social, or economic circumstances of his narrative, it should be useful here, by way of introduction, briefly to examine the historical background of fourteenth-century Rome, the personality of Cola di Rienzo and the nature of his revolution of 1347, and finally the literary characteristics of the *Life* itself.

ROME IN THE TIME OF COLA DI RIENZO[1]

"How doth the city sit solitary that was full of people? How is the mistress of the Gentiles become as a widow?" With these words Dante opened his epistle of 1314 to the Italian cardinals, quoting the first verse of *Lamentations* and using the image of a widow which was to become the standard metaphor in art and literature for mid-fourteenth-century Rome. The image was an

1 For the historical background of fourteenth-century Rome see the works by Duprè Theseider, Gregorovius, Mollat, and Morghen listed in the bibliography.

14 INTRODUCTION

apt one, for the Eternal City in this period was bereaved indeed. No Holy Roman Emperor had ruled from Rome since the time of Otto III (996-1002). The coronation ceremony of Dante's hero, the Emperor Henry VII, had ended in ignominious failure when his partisans were prevented from escorting him to the Vatican by the combined forces of the Angevin King Robert of Naples and the Guelfs of Rome in 1312. The Romans had a brief taste of glory when Louis of Bavaria was crowned Emperor by Sciarra Colonna, Captain of the People of Rome, in 1328. But the unrelenting opposition of Pope John XXII to the Bavarian soon made the citizens regret this act of rash nostalgia; and the Empire itself, already moribund, became a dead letter, at least in Italy, shortly afterward.

Much more important to Rome than the loss of the Empire, however, was the loss of the Popes. The Avignon papacy, initiated in 1305 as a temporary measure under Clement V, began to look more and more permanent, especially to the deserted Romans, as the fourteenth century wore on. Modern research has shown that the fourteenth-century Italians (not to mention many of their descendants) were wrong to believe that the Avignon popes were no more than the base slaves of the kings of France. Their prolonged absence from Rome was rather the result of a combination of accidents: the ill health of one pope or another, the complex politics of the Hundred Years' War, the projected crusade to regain Jerusalem from the Turks, and the geographical convenience of Avignon, which at this time was much closer to the center of Latin Christendom than Rome was. But national hatreds between Frenchmen and Italians played a part in this situation as well, and the long-range problems and aspirations of the transplanted Curia were of little interest to the citizens of a city forced to struggle along without its temporal and spiritual leader for so many years. The economic loss alone was incalculable : the papal court and the visitors it attracted had always been an important source of income to the Romans.

Floods, fires, famine, and earthquakes took their toll during these decades, but more destructive than any of these were Rome's own barons. The endless, anarchic struggles of the great baronial families were a major reason for the popes' reluctance to return to Rome in the first place. The inordinate power of these clans was based on their possession of vast estates and fortresses in the countryside surrounding Rome. Using these as citadels and sources of men and income, they literally tore the city to pieces in their ceaseless struggle for supremacy over one another ; Rome was packed with forts, towers, and barricades, built on and with the ruins of antiquity. The alliances of the barons were fluid, but the leaders of one party were usually the Guelf Orsini, who had prevented the Vatican coronation of Henry VII, and of the other the Ghibelline Colonna, who had seized and humiliated Pope Boniface VIII at Anagni in 1303. Ordinary citizens could of course do nothing to stop them ; merchants, farmers, and pilgrims were at their mercy. Robbery, murder, and extortion were commonplace ; the city was in constant turmoil. This, then, was the stage for the revolution of Cola di Rienzo in 1347.

COLA DI RIENZO

The name Cola di Rienzo (*Cola de Rienzi* in the dialect of Rome) means, approximately, "Nick, Larry's son." The events of the coup d'état engineered in Rome by this innkeeper's son and notary in 1347, and his brief return to power as papal Senator in 1354, are vividly described in the *Life of Cola di Rienzo* and need not be repeated here. But since the Chronicler makes little attempt to analyze his character or his politics, a brief examination of these will be in order at this point.

As a public figure Cola has been variously depicted by modern historians as a protofascist, a forerunner of Garibaldi, and even as the founder of the entire Renaissance. As an individual he has been called everything from an incompetent madman to a martyred hero.[2] Personally he will always remain an enigmatic figure : the Chronicler has almost nothing to say about his private life, and Cola's Latin letters, though autobiographical to a certain extent, are essentially public documents, written in a public style, and hence reveal little of his individual personality. But his politics, which at first sight appear so bizarre, can in fact be explained when seen in the context of his times.

Four major political and intellectual elements can be discerned in the short-lived "tribunate" Cola established in 1347.[3] First and most important is the idea of Rome. In this he was by no means unique; the belief that Rome was the *caput mundi*, with a central role to play in world politics, was shared by all Romans, even during the most abject periods of the city's history, and indeed by all Christians. The ideal of Rome was all that mattered ; political realities, such as the ruinous condition of the city itself, and the shift of political power to the north and west of Europe, could be, and generally were, ignored. But Cola's devotion to this ideal was extraordinary even among his contemporaries ; his unusually assiduous attention to the traditions and physical remains of Rome is caught by the Chronicler in his opening chapter on Cola (1.1): "Lord, what a fast reader he was ! He was well acquainted with Livy, Seneca, Cicero, and Valerius Maximus ; he loved to describe the great

---

2 For Cola as a protofascist see bibliography for Fleischer; as an abortive forerunner of Garibaldi, Gregorovius; as the founder of the Renaissance, Burdach. The accounts of Barzini, Duprè Theseider, and Morghen are much more balanced. Cola was accused of insanity even by his own contemporaries (cf. Villani 12.90); he was portrayed as a martyred hero by Byron (*Childe Harold's Pilgrimage* 4.114), Bulwer-Lytton, and Wagner.

3 For the material which follows see the works of Cosenza, Davis, Douie, Reeves, Waley, and Weiss listed in the bibliography.

deeds of Julius Caesar. Every day he would gaze at the marble engravings which lie about in Rome. He alone knew how to read the ancient inscriptions. He translated all the ancient writings ; he interpreted those marble shapes perfectly. Lord ! how often he would say, 'Where are those good Romans ? Where is their high justice ? If only I could live in such times !'" Cola's skill in communicating this enthusiasm was unparalleled ; as the Chronicler says at one point (4.4) : "... Cola de Rienzi began to speak of the power of the Romans. He wove his tales from Livy and told of Biblical deeds ; he opened the fount of his wisdom. Lord, how well he spoke ! He would exert all his skill in declamation, and would speak so effectively that everyone would be stupefied by his beautiful speeches ; he would lift each man off his feet." If Cola's eloquence could move the realistic Pope Clement VI, as well as the idealist Petrarch (cf. *Epp. Var.* 38, 40, 42, 48), and the courtiers of Charles IV in Prague as well as the young dreamer Arimbaldo de Narba, it is no wonder that his speeches could arouse the citizens of Rome, who were always so ready to believe in the grandiose pretensions of their city.

The second major element in Cola's politics was the ideal of communal government. In this, the most practical aspect of his regime, Cola was not unique even in the city of Rome. In fact, only four years before his revolution, Cola himself had gone to Avignon as ambassador of the short-lived popular government of Rome known as the "Thirteen Good Men," and this was only one of many such attempts at communal rule in the city. Communes of this sort were to be found throughout northern and central Italy during this period, where they were often much more successful and long-lasting than the attempts at Rome. Despite the misleading catchwords, such as government of "the people," used by chroniclers and politicians alike to describe these regimes, it is a mistake to think of them as anything like proletarian democracies. They were essentially republican governments of the upper middle class and minor nobility ; even major nobles might at times participate in them. The Chronicler makes it clear that this was the case with Cola's government as well ; in a description of a meeting called by Cola shortly before the coup, he says (1.4): "After this he [Cola] gathered together many discreet Roman plebeians, and good men ; there were plebeian knights as well, men of good birth, and many discreet and rich merchants." "Discreet" and "good men" are political and economic euphemisms ; modern equivalents might be such expressions as "men of substance" or "responsible citizens." The papal vicar himself participated in the revolution, and Cola often employed major barons as commanders for his armies. The ordinances of the "Good Estate," as Cola called his new government, were clearly intended to support the Church and provide a favorable atmosphere for trade and agriculture (see *Life* 1.6), and it was not until Cola began to challenge papal authority and displease the merchants with his severe taxation that he fell from power. The eventual fate of the Italian communes was to fall to the rule, known as the "seigniory," of a powerful single ruler, such as the Medici in Florence; after a long delay caused by the Great Schism of the West, Rome fell to the most powerful seigniory of all, that of the Pope.

The third element of Cola's tribunate was the goal of Italian unity. For obvious reasons this is a question which has interested modern historians immensely. But the brevity of Cola's rule makes it hard to determine how serious he was about this goal. It is true that he summoned representatives of the Italian communes to a pan-Italian synod, and on 2 August 1347 he held a "Festival of Italian Unity" in Rome, at which gifts and banners were distributed to communal envoys. But all of this may have been no more than another facet of the old Roman *caput mundi* dream. Cola's assumption of imperial trappings, and his use of imperial ceremonies — at his coronation of 15

August, for example — would suggest that the goal he had in mind was even loftier, and more impractical, than a united Italian nation. He was temporarily successful in subjecting the "district," the towns and countryside in the immediate neighborhood of the city, to Roman rule ; this is clearly described in the *Life*. But Cola's more grandiose plans and ambitions did not interest the Chronicler very much ; for example, he does not even mention the Festival of Italian Unity.

Finally, the mystical beliefs of the Fraticelli, a heretical branch of the Franciscan order, clearly played an important part in Cola's political development. What interested Cola most about the Fraticelli was not their anticlericalism or their position on ecclesiastical poverty, but their interpretation of world history. Basing their beliefs on the prophecies of the mystic philosopher Joachim, Abbot of Floris (d.1202), the Fraticelli maintained that the age of the Holy Ghost, successor to the Old Testament age of God the Father and the New Testament age of God the Son, had now arrived. Exactly what this was supposed to imply varied from one believer to another, but one common element of the new age was thought to be a more direct and personal relationship between God and man. Evidence of Cola's interest in this doctrine appears throughout the *Life*: a dove figured prominently in one of the allegorical pictures which, following a common propaganda technique of mediaeval Italy, he had painted on a church wall before his rise to power (1.4); thirty Masses of the Holy Ghost were celebrated on the eve of his revolution (1.5; the revolution itself took place on Pentecost); the words *Spiritus Sanctus* appeared on his mace, and a silver dove topped his standard (1.13); the watchword assigned before a major battle with the nobles was "Knights of the Holy Ghost" (1.32). Finally, after Cola had been driven out of office, he took refuge with a group of hermit Fraticelli in the Abruzzi mountains, where a certain Fra Angelo regaled him with magnificent prophecies concerning his return to power (4.1). Cola was not unique among fourteenth-century political leaders in his fascination with this sect; for example, Giovanni di Vico of Viterbo, one of the Tribune's worst enemies, was well known as a protector of the Fraticelli.

Thus we can see that there was nothing particularly anomalous in the politics or ideals of Cola di Rienzo. What made him special was his unparalleled rhetorical talent and his extraordinary ability to put on a good show. His two periods of power, all told, lasted for less than a year; he had no permanent effect whatever on the political development of Italy or Rome. He has become a figure of heroic legend and romantic history: a perfectly appropriate fate, and one which, we can imagine, would have pleased him immensely.

THE *LIFE OF COLA DI RIENZO*[4]

The *Life of Cola di Rienzo* was never intended to be an independent biography. It consists of four chapters taken from a larger chronicle, known to historians as the *Historiae romanae fragmenta*, which described various events occurring in Rome and elsewhere between 1327 and 1357. The four chapters of this work which deal with Cola di Rienzo have traditionally been treated as a separate biography ever since the first printed edition of the *Life* was published in Bracciano in 1624 by Andrea Fei. From internal evidence we know that the Chronicle was composed around the year 1358 ; we also know that the anonymous author, an upper-middle-class layman, studied

---

4 This analysis is drawn to a large extent from the introductory material included in Frugoni and Ghisalberti's editions of the *Life*, and from the studies of Bertoni, Castellani, Contini, Pirodda, and Ugolini listed in the bibliography.

medicine at the University of Bologna (Ch. 11 of the complete chronicle). The chronicle is written in Romanesco, the Italian dialect of Rome ; the author explains his choice of the vernacular, along with his reasons for writing history, in his Preface, which deserves to be quoted here in full.

In his Book of Etymologies [1.3] the glorious St. Isidore says that the inventor of writing was a Greek named Cadmus. Before his time writing did not exist. Hence it was impossible to record memorable deeds in writing. Instead they were recorded in stone statues and bas-reliefs, which were set up in famous places where many people could see them, or in the places where the events, such as a great battle, or victory, or disasters and defeats, actually occurred. These were sculpted in stone, and animals as well, or men in armor, as a memorial of such events. These stones were set up where the events occurred, to memorialize them forever. There were no books written because there was no writing among the Greeks at that time. And throughout Italy, in France, and especially in Rome, the Romans did the same: to make their deeds known to posterity, they built triumphal arches, which depicted battles, armed men, horses, etc., such as are found in **** and in Rimini.

After Cadmus invented writing, people began to write things down which would otherwise be forgotten, especially magnificent and illustrious deeds. Thus Livy wrote the history of Rome from the foundation of the city to the time of Octavian; thus Lucan wrote about the deeds of the Caesars ; thus Sallust, and many other writers, recorded in literature the past events of Rome.

So how can I, who have witnessed (thanks to God) events so memorable for their outstanding novelty in this world, allow such events to pass by without writing about them ? Indeed it would hardly be fitting to leave them shrouded in obscurity because of laziness. Therefore I wish to make a special book and narrative. This is a huge and noble task, and I am undertaking it for several reasons. First, the reader may find things written here which will recur in similar fashion in the future, and thus come to know the truth of Solomon's words, "Nothing under the sun is new; that which appears to be new has happened before" [cf. *Eccle.* 1:10]. Second, the reader will find many noble and excellent examples here, which will help him to avoid dangers and emulate virtue. Third, I am impressed by the magnificence of these events, as I said above. A man cares nothing for little things ; he leaves them alone. He writes about big things. My fourth reason is one which influenced Livy. In his first decade [9.17-19] he mentions Alexander of Macedon; he tells how many infantrymen and cavalrymen he had, how long his empire lasted, and how extensive it was. And he says that Alexander's greatness was nothing compared to that of the Romans. In saying this he answers a question which could have been put as follows: "Why are you bothering with the deeds of Alexander when you are writing the history of the Romans?" Livy answers, "I am doing this to put my mind at rest." That is to say, my mind has been stirred to write about this material; I wish to discuss it, and then my mind will be at ease. So say I: my mind has been stirred up, and it will not rest until I record in writing the beautiful deeds and events which I have seen during my life. My fifth reason is also one which Livy mentions. In the preface of the first book of the first decade [*Praef.* 5], he says, "While I am occupied in writing these things, I am remote, and do not see the cruelties which our city has witnessed for so long a time." So say I: while I am enjoying this work, I am remote, and I do not experience the wars and the hardships which overrun the country, and which, because of their great tribulations, bring sorrow and misery not only to those who suffer them, but to those who hear of them as well. This is the absolute truth.

And may God be my witness, and my contemporaries as well, that what is written below is the truth. I saw these events and heard them. In particular I gathered information about certain events which occurred in my own country from trustworthy people who were unanimous in what they told me. Therefore I shall place certain signs at appropriate places in my text, which will reassure the reader and free me from suspicion in what I say.

Furthermore I am writing this Chronicle in the vernacular, so that it may be useful to everyone who can read simple texts, such as common merchants, and many other excellent people, who are not students of literature. Therefore for the common utility and delight I have composed this work in the vernacular, although I have already written it in Latin. But that work was not so well organized nor so copious as this one. Also I am dividing this work into chapters, so that whoever wishes to find beautiful things in it will be able to do so easily.

The opening statements of this Preface, including the careless citation of Isidore (who in fact says that the Hebrews, not Cadmus, were the inventors of writing) are mediaeval commonplaces. More humanistic, however, are the two references to Livy, whereby the Chronicler suggests that basically he is writing history for its own sake. The absence of any statement about the workings of the hand of God in human history is also noteworthy. Theocentric explanations of history were a standing rule in earlier mediaeval chronicles, and their use was continued by the two great Florentine chroniclers of the fourteenth century, Dino Compagni and Giovanni Villani. Our author, by contrast, seems almost completely secular in his approach to human affairs, both in the *Life* and in the surviving chapters of the remainder of his chronicle. An apparent exception (unique in the *Life*[5]) to this rule occurs in 3.1, where it is stated that "After Pope Innocent's election God wreaked a terrible vengeance on those who had seized the Senate of Rome from him" ; the death by stoning of Vertuollo delli Orzini, senator of Rome, is then

---

5 The most notable exception to this rule in the remainder of the chronicle occurs in Ch. 9, where the miraculous reward of a landowner who was generous to the poor during a famine is described, and the Chronicler comments, "Thus God clearly showed how well He is pleased with magnanimous charity in times of need." But here he is explaining a miracle, an isolated, non-political event.

described. But here God, almost like a Homeric deity, is responding to a personal insult, the usurpation of His Vicar's power, rather than preserving the moral order of the universe. Hence the Chronicler's apparently incongruous attempt to explain this through the *exemplum* of Dionysius of Syracuse's punishment for desecrating his pagan idols turns out not to be so far off the mark after all.

What in fact seems to interest and impress the Chronicler the most is not morality or theology but heroism, heroic self-assertion, of any sort. For example, we would expect him, as a good burgess, to be all in favor of Cola's middle-class revolution against the rapacious Roman barons, but this is not the case. Though he realizes the importance of Cola's government for the freedom of the Roman people, stating at the one point (4.13) that "only with this man could they [the Romans] find liberty," his sympathy for the Tribune vanishes almost completely as soon as he begins to show signs of cowardice or weakness. And he reserves his highest praise for the heroic, but thoroughly antisocial, *condottiere* Fra Morreale (4.11): "from the time of Caesar to the present day there has never been a better man."

The *Life* as we have it is the result of a historical accident, and, equally by accident, it presents an interestingly balanced structure. The first and last books describe the rise and fall of Cola di Rienzo. The second and third books, included in the traditional selection only because Cola happens to be mentioned briefly in each of them, provide illuminating contrasts to Cola's story: the second, with its portrait of the Roman mob which will eventually destroy Cola and which is so far removed from Cola's vision of the noble Romans of antiquity, and the third, with its description of the deeds of Cardinal Albornoz, the Papal Legate, who, unlike Cola, was realistic, efficient, and ultimately successful in subduing the rebellious robber barons of central Italy. Because of the depth and breadth which they add to the Chronicler's portrait of Cola and mediaeval Rome (subjects which have all too often been misleadingly viewed in historical isolation), as well as for their great intrinsic interest, these two books have been included in this translation.

Since many chapters of the complete chronicle are missing, it is hard to say anything about the overall structure of the work. But the table of contents, which does survive, does not suggest much organization or basic unity. Nor does the Chronicler make any real attempt to provide historical explanations of his material, or even to find the most elementary logical connections between the events he narrates. His strength lies rather in his treatment of individual episodes, such as the battle at the Porta San Lorenzo (1.32-36), the death of the Papal Legate, Cardinal Annibaldo di Ceccano (2.3), and the trial and execution of Fra Morreale (4.11). In such scenes his narrative is vivid, concrete, and rapid: sometimes hilariously obscene, sometimes unbearably moving.

It is a mistake to believe, as many commentators have, that the *Life of Cola di Rienzo* is the work of an amiable primitive who happened to have a good eye for detail. Its author was an educated and literate man, who employed sophisticated rhetorical techniques, such as alliteration, assonance, etymological puns, and careful manipulation of prose rhythm and shifts in stylistic level, throughout his chronicle. The following extract, taken from the famous passage describing the death of Cola (4.13), will illustrate how some of these techniques are evident even in translation; Cola is trapped in the Palace of the Campidoglio, which is being attacked by a mob:

> The Tribune in despair placed himself in the hands of fortune. Standing in the courtyard in front of the Cancellaria, he took off his helmet and put it on again and again. This was because he had two different plans. The first plan was to die honorably, dressed in his armor, with his sword in his hand, like a magnificent and

imperial person. And this he showed when he put on his helmet and took up his arms. The second plan was to save his life and not die. And this he showed when he took off his helmet. These two desires fought with each other in his mind. The winner was the desire to save himself and live. He was a man like any other; he was afraid to die.

Then he deliberated on the best possible way of keeping himself alive; he searched and found the way, a shameful and spiritless way. By this time the Romans had thrown fire on the first gate, wood, oil, and pitch. The gate was burning; the roof of the loggia was blazing; the second gate was burning and the roof and the timbers were falling piece by piece. The noise was horrible.

The Tribune decided to pass through the fire in disguise and mingle with the others and save his life. This was his final plan. He found no other way. And so he stripped off his noble insignia; he threw away all his armor. It is a sorrowful thing to relate! He snipped off his beard and tinted his face with black coloring. Nearby there was a little lodge where the porter slept. He went in there and took an old cloak of vile cloth, of the sort shepherds wear in the Campagna. He dressed himself in this vile cloak ; then he put a coverlet from the bed over his head and thus disguised he went down. He passed the gate, which was burning; he passed the stairway and the roof tower, which was falling; he passed the last gate freely. The fire did not touch him; he mingled with the others in his changed form. He changed his accent and spoke like a peasant and said, "Up, up to the traitor!"

Note how, in the first paragraph, the battle within Cola's will (obviously imaginary, since the Tribune was alone at this point) is clearly marked by parallel phrases: "The first plan was ...", "And this he showed ..."; "The second plan was ...", "And this he showed ..." and then capped with the great sentence, detached and humane at the same time: "He was a man like any other; he was afraid to die." In the second paragraph, with a terrifying effectiveness, the Chronicler cuts suddenly to the mob;

INTRODUCTION 27

his picture of the attack is made concrete by his inclusion of physical detail ("wood, oil, and pitch"); imminent disaster is emphasized by echoing verbs: "... was burning," "... was blazing," "... was burning," "... were falling"; again the description is capped with a short, solid sentence: "The noise was horrible." Finally, in the third paragraph, the moral degeneration of the Tribune is illustrated by a corresponding physical degeneration in face and form (these details are taken up almost point for point in the contrasting *exemplum* from the history of ancient Rome with which the Chronicler concludes this chapter). The explosive personal comment which punctuates this description ("It is a sorrowful thing to relate!"), though it appears naive to the modern reader, is a standard feature of late-mediaeval historical style. Cola's doomed progress is then presented in parallel verb forms: "He passed ..., which was burning," "he passed ..., which was falling," "he passed ..." And as the climax of the entire passage (and this is again probably imaginary, since it is unlikely that anyone would have noticed such a detail at the time), the greatest orator of his day becomes his own betrayer and speaks what turn out to be his last words in the despised accent of the countryside: "Up, up to the traitor!" ("*Suso, suso a gliu traditore!*"). How deliberate and highly wrought all these effects are we can see by comparing a bald, brief sentence describing a similar escape from the Campidoglio in an earlier chapter (3.1): "His fellow Senator ingloriously saved himself by sliding down a rope and passing through the postern gate of the Palace with his face veiled and a worn-out cap on his head."

The account of the death of Cola also provides some excellent examples of the weaknesses of the Chronicler as a historian. As we know from other sources, his date for the riot is off by a year and a month. Though it is clear from the evidence he himself gives that the riot was the result of a deliberate plot by the surviving members of the Colonna family (the rioters come from regions of Rome which favor the Colonna, Cola's corpse is hung by San Marcello, near the Colonna Palace, etc.), it never occurs to the Chronicler to give us this obvious explanation; his riot comes like a bolt from the blue, foreshadowed only by Cola's increasing moral and mental degeneration. The "evidence" that Cola dabbled in witchcraft and planned to tax the Romans at an almost confiscatory level was surely forged by his enemies after his death, but the Chronicler says nothing about this. He is, in short (like his hero Livy), more of an epic poet than a historian, and the narrative and dramatic strength of episodes such as the one just examined from his *Life of Cola di Rienzo* make it an epic masterpiece of fourteenth-century Italian literature.

NOTE ON THE TRANSLATION

My translation is based on the text of *La vita di Cola di Rienzo* edited by A. M. Ghisalberti (Rome 1928); I have also employed a number of emendations suggested in the works of F. A. Ugolini and A. Frugoni (see bibliography), to whom I am indebted for the information contained in several of the footnotes as well. All geographical names have been put in the form most common in current English, as have all names of persons from classical antiquity. The names of fourteenth-century Italians, however, have been left in the form and spelling of the Romanesco dialect. The short chapters into which the books are divided, and the headings which precede these chapters, are not part of the original text but date from the later Renaissance; the headings therefore show occasional minor variations in the spelling of names. I have tried to keep the notes down to the minimum needed to comprehend the text; readers interested in further information about the people and places named in the *Life* should consult the Index and its prefatory note.

THE LIFE OF
COLA DI RIENZO

BOOK ONE

THE LIFE OF COLA DE RIENZI, ROMAN, VALOROUS CAPTAIN,
WITH ALL THE VALIANT DEEDS HE DID AGAINST THE POWERFUL
BARONS OF ROME, AND OF THE JOURNEY HE MADE TO POPE
CLEMENT IN AVIGNON. READ, READ, THAT I MAY MAKE YOU
LIFT YOUR EYEBROWS AT HIS PROWESS.

CHAPTER ONE

Parents, birth, character, and profession of Cola di Rienzo; origin of his ideas; his embassy to Pope Clement in Avignon and his return.

Cola de Rienzi was of low birth: his father was an innkeeper named Rienzi; his mother, named Matalena, earned her living by washing clothes and carrying water. He was born in the region of Regola; his house was at the riverside, among the mills, on the street leading to the Regola, behind San Tommaso, below the Jews' temple. From his youth he was nourished on the milk of eloquence: a good grammarian, an excellent speaker, and a good scholar. Lord, what a fast reader he was! He was well acquainted with Livy, Seneca, Cicero, and Valerius Maximus; he loved to describe the great deeds of Julius Caesar. Every day he would gaze at the marble engravings which lie about in Rome. He alone knew how to read the ancient inscriptions. He translated all the ancient writings; he interpreted those marble shapes perfectly. Lord! how often he would say, "Where are those good Romans? Where is their high justice? If only I could live in such times!" He was a handsome man, and on his mouth a strange smile was always appearing. He was a notary. It happened that a brother of his was killed, and no vengeance was taken for his death; Cola could do nothing to help him. He thought for a long time of avenging his brother's death; he thought for a long time of rescuing the ill-governed city of Rome.

He arranged to be sent to Avignon as ambassador to Pope Clement on behalf of the government of the Thirteen Good Men of Rome.[1] The speech he made there was so excellent and beautiful that Pope Clement loved him at once. The Pope marvelled at the beautiful style of Cola's language; he wanted to see him every day. Then Cola spoke to him at length, saying that the barons of Rome were highway robbers; they allowed homicides, robberies, adulteries, and every sort of crime; they were responsible for their city's ravaged condition. On hearing these things the Pope became angry at the nobles. But then at the petition of Cardinal Janni della Colonna, Cola fell into such disgrace, such poverty, such infirmity, that he might as well have been a pauper at a hospital. With his little coat on his back he stood in the sun like a snake. But he who brought him low raised him up: Messer Janni della Colonna brought him back before the Pope.[2] He was restored to favor and made Notary of the Chamber of Rome, with plenty of emoluments and benefits. He returned to Rome very quickly, muttering threats between his teeth.

CHAPTER TWO

In an assembly Cola makes a speech sharply criticizing the officials and rulers of the people of Rome; for this he is struck on the cheek by Andreozzo Colonna. He also admonishes the people with a mysterious picture.

After he returned from the Papal Court, Cola began to perform his office courteously; and he recognized clearly the rob-

1 This embassy, which took place in 1342-43, is described in greater detail in Ch. 12 of the complete chronicle. The ambassadors succeeded in persuading Pope Clement VI to declare 1350 a Jubilee year; the joyful letter in which Cola announced this to the Romans still survives (A. Gabrielli, ed., *Epistolario* 1).

2 It is generally agreed that Cola was restored to favor through the intervention of Petrarch, who was a protégé of the Colonna family.

beries of the dogs of the Campidoglio, the cruelty and injustice of the nobles; he saw how great the danger to the Commune was, but he could not find a good citizen who was willing to help him. Therefore he rose to his feet one time in the Assembly of Rome, where all the councillors were, and said, "You are not good citizens; you suck the blood of the poor people and refuse to help them." Then he criticized the officials and rulers for neglecting the good estate[3] of Rome. When Cola de Rienzi's eloquent speech was finished, one of the Colonna, named Andreuozzo de Normanno, who was then Chamberlain, rose up and gave him a resounding slap; then a man named Tomao de Fortifiocca, a scribe of the Senate, rose up and made the tail at him.[4] Such was the result of his speech.

Cola further admonished the rulers and the people with an image which he had painted on the Palace of the Campidoglio in front of the market. On the outer wall above the Chamber he had a picture painted of a tremendous sea, with horrible waves, storming violently. In its midst a ship was foundering, without rudder or sail. In the endangered ship was a widow woman, dressed in black, bound in a belt of mourning, her gown ripped from her breast, her hair torn, as if she would weep. She was kneeling, her hands piously crossed over her breast, as if praying to be saved from her danger. The inscription said, "This is Rome." Around the ship in the lower part of the water were four sunken ships, their sails fallen, masts broken, rudders lost. In each was a woman, sunken and dead. The first was named Babylon, the second Carthage, the third Troy, and the fourth Jerusalem. The inscription said, "Because of injustice these cities were endangered and fell." Among the dead women these words were written:

3 The "Good Estate" (*buono stato*) became Cola's catchword for his government and its aims.
4 An obscene gesture still used in Italy and the United States.

> Once you held dominion over all;
> Now here we await your fall.

On the left were two islands. On one was a woman, sitting in shame; the inscription said, "This is Italy." This woman was speaking the following words:

> You took away the power of every nation,
> And you kept me alone as your sister.

On the other island were four women with their hands on their cheeks and on their knees in an attitude of great sorrow, and they were saying:

> Once you were attended by every virtue;
> Now you wander abandoned through the sea.

These were the four Cardinal Virtues: Temperance, Justice, Prudence, and Courage. On a small island on the right a woman was kneeling and stretching her hand up to heaven, as if in prayer. She was dressed in white: she was named the Christian Faith. Her verse went:

> O greatest father, leader, and my lord,
> If Rome should perish, where then shall I stand?

On the upper right were four rows of different animals with wings who were holding horns to their mouths and blowing as if they were winds who made the sea rage and endangered the foundering ship. In the first row were lions, wolves, and bears. The inscription said, "These are the powerful barons and evil leaders." In the second were dogs, pigs, and roebucks. The inscription said, "These are the bad councillors, followers of the nobles." In the third were lambs, dragons, and foxes. The inscription said, "These are the plebeians, robbers, murderers, adulterers, and plunderers." In the fourth row, on top, were hares, cats, goats, and monkeys. The inscription said, "These are the false officials, judges, and notaries." Above was Heaven; in the middle stood the Divine Majesty, as if come in judgment. Two swords came out of His mouth, in one direction and the other. On one side stood St. Peter, on the other St. Paul, both praying. When the people saw this allegorical image, everyone was amazed.

CHAPTER THREE

At another time in St. John Lateran he admonishes the people with a speech describing the authority formerly granted by the Roman people to the Emperor Vespasian, and also with mysterious figures.

Cola de Rienzi did not use a goose quill when he wrote but a pen of fine silver. He said that his office was so noble that his pen ought to be of silver. Soon afterward he admonished the people with a beautiful speech in the vernacular, which he delivered in St. John Lateran, behind the choir. He had a magnificent metal tablet[5] fixed to the wall, with ancient letters written on it, which he alone knew how to read and interpret. Around this tablet he had a picture painted, showing how the Roman Senate conceded authority to the Emperor Vespasian. There in the middle of the church he had a speaker's platform built of planks, and high wooden seats, decorated with tapestries and bunting. He gathered many Roman nobles together, among whom were Stefano della Colonna and his son, Janni Colonna, who was one of the most clever and magnificent men of Rome. There were many learned men as well, judges and canon

5 An ancient bronze tablet containing the *Lex Regia* of Vespasian; Cola's interpretation of its contents was, to say the least, very free.

lawyers, and many other people of authority. Cola de Rienzi
mounted his pulpit among these notable people. He was dressed
in a cloak and a German cape, and a hood of fine white cloth;
on his head he wore a white hat, with a circle of golden crowns
around the brim; from the upper part of the hat arose a naked
silver sword, the point of which went into the foremost crown
and divided it in the middle.

He climbed up eagerly; silence was called for, and he made
his beautiful discourse, his beautiful speech, and said that Rome
had fallen and lay overthrown on the ground, and could not see
where she lay, since her eyes had been torn from her head. The
eyes were the Pope and the Emperor, whom Rome had lost
because of her citizens' iniquity.[6] Then he said, "You see how
great was the magnificence of the Senate, which gave authority
to the Empire." He had a paper read which contained the articles describing the authority which the people of Rome conceded to the Emperor Vespasian: he could make laws and
treaties at will with any nation or people; he could decrease or
increase the garden of Rome, that is, Italy; he could grant a
greater or lesser fief, as he wished; he could promote men to the
status of duke or king, and demote and degrade them; he could
destroy cities and rebuild them; he could divert the courses of
rivers; and he could impose taxes and remit them at will. All
these things the people of Rome conceded to Vespasian just as
they had conceded them to Tiberius Caesar. When this paper
had been read, and these articles, he said, "Gentlemen, so great
was the majesty of the people of Rome that it gave authority to
the Emperor. Now we have lost it, to our great injury and
shame." Then he continued, "Romans, you do not have peace;
your lands are not ploughed. Though in fact the Jubilee is ap-

6 This image was also used by Petrarch, in a verse letter addressed (ca.
1335) to Pope Benedict XII (*Ep. metr.* 1.2.158).

proaching, you are not provided with food or provisions, and if the people who come to the Jubilee find no food here, in their ravenous hunger they will seize the very stones of Rome. And even the stones are not enough for such a multitude." Then he concluded, saying, "I pray for you that you will have peace with one another." Then he added these words: "Gentlemen, I know that many people vilify me for what I say and do, and why is this? Because of envy. But I thank God that there are three things which consume themselves in the same way. The first is luxury, the second is fire, and the third is envy." When he had finished his speech and descended from the throne, he was praised warmly by all the people.

CHAPTER FOUR

The barons of Rome mock Cola. With a picture at Sant'Angelo in Pescheria, and in other ways, he predicts his ascendancy, and holds a meeting for the reform of the state.

In these days when he attended banquets with Janni Colonna and the nobles of Rome, the barons made fun of his speech-making. They made him rise to his feet and address them, and he said, "I shall be a great lord, or emperor; I'll persecute all these barons; this one I'll torture, that one I'll behead." He con-demned all of them. At this the barons burst out laughing.

Then he predicted his ascendancy and his reform of the government of the city in this way: on the wall of Sant'Angelo in Pescheria, a place famous throughout the world,[7] he had a picture painted. In the left-hand corner of the picture was a brightly burning fire, with smoke and flames going up to

7 This church still stands, though it could no longer be called "famous throughout the world"; it is built in the ruins of the Portico of Octavia.

heaven. In this fire were many plebeians and rulers, some of whom appeared half alive, and others dead; and in this same fire was an aged woman; two parts of her body were burnt and blackened, while the third part remained unharmed. In the right-hand corner was a church, out of which an armed angel, dressed in white, was coming; his cloak was of scarlet vermilion; in his hand he was carrying a naked sword; with his left hand he was taking the aged woman by the hand, as if to free her from danger. At the top of the bell tower of the church St. Peter and St. Paul were standing, as if they had come from heaven, and they were saying:

Angel, angel, help our hostess.

Then the picture showed many falcons, looking as if they had fallen from heaven; they were falling dead in the midst of the raging fire. High up in heaven there was a beautiful white dove, with a crown of myrtle in its beak, which it was giving to a tiny sparrow-like bird; then the dove drove the falcons from heaven. The little bird was carrying the crown and placing it on the head of the old woman. Below these pictures was written, "The time of great justice is coming, and you await the time." The people poured into Sant'Angelo and looked at these pictures; many said that they were meaningless and laughed at them. Others said, "It will take more than pictures to reform the government of Rome." Others said, "This is a great thing, and it has great significance." He also predicted his ascendancy in the following way: he wrote a placard and put it up on the door of San Giorgio della Chiavica.[8] The placard read, "In a short time the Romans will return to their ancient Good Estate." This sign was posted on the first day of Lent on the door of San Giorgio della Chiavica.

8 Now called San Giorgio in Velabro.

After this he gathered together many discreet Roman plebeians, and good men; there were plebeian knights as well, men of good birth, and many discreet and rich merchants. He had a meeting with them, and discussed the government of the city. Finally he gathered these good and mature people together on the Aventine Hill, and in a secret place a discussion was held about their intentions for the Good Estate. He rose to his feet among them and, weeping, spoke of the misery, the servitude, and the danger in which the city of Rome lay. He also spoke of the peaceful and illustrious government which the Romans used to have; he spoke of the faithful obedience of the surrounding lands. Saying, "These things are lost," he wept and made the people weep bitterly. Then he concluded, saying that peace and justice had to be preserved, and comforted them. He said, "Do not worry about money. The Chamber of Rome has many inestimable revenues. First, the hearth tax is four soldi per fire: from the Ponte di Ceperano to the Ponte della Paglia this amounts to a hundred thousand florins. Further, from the salt tax, one hundred thousand florins; also, from the gates and castles of Rome, one hundred thousand florins; also, from the tax on cattle and from fines, one hundred thousand florins." Then he said, "For the present we shall begin with four thousand florins, which my lord the Pope has sent, with the full knowledge of his vicar." Then he said, "Gentlemen, do not believe that it is with the permission of the Pope that many citizens do violence to the goods of the Church." With these words he kindled the spirit of the group. He went on to speak of many things, which brought tears to the eyes of his listeners. Then he discussed his plans for the Good Estate, and concerning this he administered a written oath to each man.

CHAPTER FIVE

Description of the condition of Rome in those times. Cola reveals himself as chief of the reform of the government of Rome. He comes armed to the Campidoglio and addresses the people.

Meanwhile the city of Rome was in agony. It had no rulers; men fought every day; robbers were everywhere; nuns were insulted; there was no refuge; little girls were assaulted and led away to dishonor; wives were taken from their husbands in their very beds; farmhands going out to work were robbed, and where? in the very gates of Rome; pilgrims, who had come to the holy churches for the good of their souls, were not protected, but were murdered and robbed; even the priests were criminals. Everywhere lust, everywhere evil, no justice, no law; there was no longer any escape; everyone was dying; the man who was strongest with the sword was most in the right. A person's only hope was to defend himself with the help of his relatives and friends; every day groups of armed men were formed.

The nobles and barons were not in Rome. Messer Stefano della Colonna had gone with the militia to Corneto for grain; this was at the end of the month of April. Then Cola de Rienzi, on the first day,[9] sent out a trumpeter with a proclamation asking every man to come unarmed to the Good Estate at the sound of the bell. The following day, after midnight, he heard thirty Masses of the Holy Ghost in the church of Sant'Angelo in Pescheria. Then, at the hour of mid-tierce, he left the church, completely armed, except for his head, which was uncovered. He went out nobly and publicly; a crowd of soldiers followed him, all shouting. Before him he had three men of his conspiracy

9 19 May 1347; the next day was Pentecost.

carry three banners. The first was very large, red with gold letters; on it was painted Rome, sitting between two lions, with the
world in her left hand and a palm in her right. This was the
banner of liberty; Cola Guallato, the good speaker, carried it.
The second was white; on it was St. Paul, holding a sword and
the crown of justice. This was carried by Stefaniello, called
Magnacuccia, a notary. On the third was St. Peter with the keys
of concord and peace. Another man carried the banner of St.
George the Cavalier ; because it was old it was carried in a case
on a spear.

Now Cola de Rienzi, though still somewhat fearful, gathered
his courage and set out, together with the Pope's vicar, and
climbed to the Palace of the Campidoglio in the year of our Lord
thirteen forty-six.[10] He had a force of about one hundred armed
men. A huge crowd of people gathered, and Cola mounted the
platform and made an eloquent speech on the misery and servitude of the people of Rome. He said that he was exposing his
person to danger for the love of the Pope and the salvation of
the people of Rome.

CHAPTER SIX

*On the Campidoglio Cola publishes the laws for implementing
the good government of Rome. On account of this the people
proclaim him lord with absolute power, and he remains on the
Campidoglio with the Pope's vicar.*

Then he had a document read which contained the ordinances
of the Good Estate. Conte, son of Cecco Mancino, read them
out. These were some of the clauses :

10 Actually 1347; the Pope's vicar was Raimond de Chameyrac, Bishop of
Orvieto.

First, that every person who kills should himself be killed, without exception.

Second, that lawsuits should not be prolonged, but should be settled within fifteen days.

Third, that houses in Rome should not be torn down for any reason, but should become the property of the Commune.[11]

Fourth, that in each region of Rome there should be kept one hundred infantrymen and twenty-five cavalrymen at the expense of the Commune, and that they each should be provided with a shield worth five silver carlins and an appropriate stipend.

Fifth, that orphans and widows should have assistance from the Chamber of the Commune of Rome.

Sixth, that in the Roman swamps and ponds and on the Roman seashores a boat should be continually maintained for the protection of merchants.

Seventh, that the money from the hearth tax, salt tax, gates, tolls, and fines should be spent, if necessary, for the Good Estate.

Eighth, that the castles, bridges, ports, gates, and fortresses of Rome should not be guarded by any baron, but only by the leader of the people.

Ninth, that no noble might have a fortress.

Tenth, that the barons should keep the roads secure, and not harbor robbers and criminals, and that they should provide provisions for Rome under penalty of one thousand silver marks.

Eleventh, that assistance should be given to the monasteries from the treasury of the Commune.

Twelfth, that in each region of Rome there should be a granary, and that grain should be procured when required.

Thirteenth, that any Roman killed in battle while serving the Commune should have, if an infantryman, an indemnity of one hundred pounds, and if a cavalryman one hundred florins.

11 Ordinarily the houses of convicted criminals were torn down.

Fourteenth, that the cities and towns within the district of the city of Rome should be ruled by the people of Rome.

Fifteenth, that anyone who makes an accusation and does not prove it should sustain the penalty which the accused would have suffered, whether in his person or in money.

Many other things were written in this document; the people were extremely pleased with it, and they all raised their hands in the air, and joyfully elected him their lord, but with the Pope's vicar as his colleague. They also gave him freedom to punish, to execute, to pardon, to appoint officers, to make laws and treaties with neighboring peoples, and to establish boundaries. They also gave him pure and free imperial power for as far as the jurisdiction of the Roman people extended.[12]

CHAPTER SEVEN

Stefano della Colonna returns to Rome, angry at Cola because of these events, and threatens him. He is, however, ordered to leave Rome, as are all the barons; this they do. And Cola has himself confirmed by the people, and obtains for himself and the Pope's vicar the titles of Tribunes and liberators of the people.

News of these events in Rome soon reached the ears of Messer Stefano della Colonna, who was in Corneto with the militia to gather grain. He immediately rode off with a small company and came to Rome. As he entered the Piazza di San Marcello, he announced that he was not pleased with what had happened. Early the next morning Cola de Rienzi sent Messer Stefano an edict ordering him to leave Rome. Messer Stefano took the note and tore it into a thousand pieces, saying, "If this madman

12 This is a paraphrase of the formula used for conferring power on the Holy Roman Emperor at his coronation.

provokes me any further I'll have him thrown out of the windows of the Campidoglio." When Cola de Rienzi heard this, he had the alarm bell sounded at once. All the people gathered in a rage; the situation seemed very dangerous. Messer Stefano mounted his horse and with only a single foot soldier fled from Rome. He scarcely had time to stop for a moment at San Lorenzo fuori le Mura to eat a little bread. The old man went to his son and grandson at Palestrina and complained bitterly.

Then Cola de Rienzi sent an edict to all the barons of Rome, ordering them to leave the city and go to their castles; this was done at once. The following day all the bridges within the circuit of the city were surrendered to him. Then Cola de Rienzi appointed officers, and arrested one man after another; he tortured some and beheaded others without mercy; he judged all the defendants severely. Then he addressed the people; at this assembly he had himself and all his acts confirmed, and asked as a favor from the people that he and the Pope's vicar be called Tribunes of the People and liberators.

CHAPTER EIGHT

The barons conspire against Cola, but can reach no agreement. They are, however, summoned and forced by him to swear to support the good government of Rome; the judges and notaries do likewise.

Then the lords wished to conspire against the Tribune and the Good Estate, but they could not reach an agreement; the thing remained undone. When Cola de Rienzi heard that the plot of the barons had failed because of their discord, he summoned them and sent them the edict. The first to obey was Stefano della Colonna, son of Messer Stefano. He went into the Palace with a few men and saw that justice was administered to all people. There were many people in the Campidoglio; he was afraid and filled with wonder at such a multitude. The Tribune appeared before him in armor, and made him swear on the Body of Christ and on the Gospel not to oppose the Tribune and the Romans, and to provide grain, to keep the roads secure, not to harbor robbers or criminals, to help orphans and wards, not to cheat the Commune of its goods, and to appear armed or unarmed whenever ordered. When Stefano was dismissed, look! there came Messer Ranallo delli Orsini, then Jordano, then Messer Stefano the father. To make a long story short, all the barons fearfully swore to submit to the Good Estate, and offered their own persons, fortresses, and vassals for the defense of the city. Francesco de Saviello was the Tribune's own liege lord; nevertheless he too came to swear obedience.

Meanwhile the Tribune preserved justice severely, without mercy; he even beheaded a monk of Sant'Anastasio, an infamous person. The outer garments of the Tribune were of a bright, fiery scarlet; his face and appearance were terrifying. He gave well-ordered replies to so many people, that a man would scarcely have believed that he had had time to understand what the requests were. A few days later the judges of the city came and swore fidelity and offered themselves to the Good Estate. Then the notaries came and did the same, then the merchants. In short, one by one, peacefully, unarmed, every man came and swore to the Good Estate. Soon everyone began to approve of these things, and armed conflict began to cease.

CHAPTER NINE

Cola establishes the House of Justice and Peace for the reconciliation of disputes, and administers justice so diligently that every evildoer flees in terror. In these times a monster is born in Rome.

For these things the Tribune established the House of Justice and Peace and set up in it the banner of St. Paul, on which the naked sword and the palm of victory were depicted, and assigned to it the most just plebeians, who were in charge of peace, the good men who were the Peacemakers. This was the procedure followed there: two enemies came in and gave guarantees of making peace; then, when the nature of the injury had been established, the man who had done it suffered just what he had done to the victim. Then they kissed each other on the mouth, and the offended man gave complete peace. A man had blinded another in one eye; he came and was led up the steps of the Campidoglio and knelt there. The man who had been deprived of an eye came; the malefactor wept and prayed in God's name that he pardon him. Then he stretched out his face for him to draw out his eye, if he wanted to. The second man did not blind him, but was moved by pity; he forgave him his injury. Civil suits were likewise settled promptly.

At this time a horrible fear entered the minds of robbers, murderers, malefactors, adulterers, and every person of evil repute. Every infamous person left the city surreptitiously, and the criminals fled secretly; they were afraid that they would be seized in their own houses and dragged off to punishment. So the guilty ones fled beyond the boundaries of the Roman countryside. They looked to no one for protection; they left their houses, fields, vineyards, wives, and children. Then the forests began to flourish because no robbers were found in them. Then the oxen began to plough; the pilgrims began to seek out the sanctuaries; the merchants began to travel and go about their business.

At this time in the city of Rome a monster was born: in the quarter of Camigliano[13] a soldier's wife gave birth to a stillborn infant which had two heads, four hands, and four feet, as if there were two infants attached at the chest. Though one was larger than the other, it appeared that the smaller was overpowering the larger, much to the wonder of the people. Meanwhile fear and terror assailed the tyrants; the good people, as if freed from slavery, rejoiced.

CHAPTER TEN

The Tribune sends letters to the Pope and all the princes of Europe concerning his ascendancy and government.

Then the Tribune called a general council and wrote eloquent letters to the cities and communes of Tuscany, Lombardy, Campagna, Romagna, and Marittima; to the Doge of Venice; to Messer Lucchino, Tyrant of Milan; to the Marquises of Ferrara, to the Holy Father Pope Clement, to Louis, Duke of Bavaria, who had been elected Emperor, as was said above;[14] and to the Princes of Naples. To these letters he prefixed his name, with a magnificent title, in the following form: "Nicola the severe and clement, Tribune of liberty, peace, and justice, and illustrious liberator of the sacred Roman republic." In these letters he declared the good, peaceful, and just estate which he had begun. He declared how the way to Rome, which used to be dangerous,

13 An area of Rome near the Pantheon, so called from a monument known as the Arch of Camillus.
14 In Ch. 4 (now lost) of the complete chronicle.

was free. He asked them to send him accredited syndics, whom he needed to discuss things useful to the Good Estate in the Roman Synod. Then he urged that they be of good cheer and give praise and thanks to God for so great a benefit.[15]

The couriers who carried his letters held silver-plated wooden rods in their hands; they were unarmed. These couriers of his so multiplied that there was soon a great number of them, since they were received graciously, and everyone paid them great honor, and they were given gifts.

One of his couriers, a Florentine, was sent to Avignon to see the Pope and Cardinal Janni della Colonna ; he carried a linen purse enameled with the finest silver, and a wooden rod enameled with the finest silver, bearing the arms of the people of Rome, and of the Pope, and of the Tribune, worth thirty florins. When he returned to Rome, the courier said, "I have carried this staff publicly through the woods and through the streets; thousands of people have knelt before it and kissed it with tears of joy for the safe highways, free of robbers."

The Tribune had many writers and scribes who kept writing letters day and night. Many were the most famous of the district of Rome. Then jesters began to gather about him, and courtiers, sonneteers, and singers; poems and popular songs were composed relating his deeds.

CHAPTER ELEVEN

The Tribune hangs Martino di Porto, a tyrannical aristocrat, to frighten the others.

At this time in Rome there lived a noble young aristocrat named Martino de Puorto, nephew of the Cardinal of Ceccano

15 This paragraph is an accurate summary of the letters Cola sent to various Italian cities announcing his new government; see *Epistolario* 2-5.

and of Cardinal Javoco Gaetano; formerly he had been Senator.
His ancestors had held the office of Senator many times. This
Martino was mentioned earlier in the account of the stranded
galley.[16] He was Lord of the Castle of Porto. He led the life of a
tyrant, and disgraced his nobility with tyrannies and robberies.
He married a most noble woman, Madonna Mascia delli Alberteschi, a beautiful widow. He lived with this new wife of his for
about a month, since he could not keep away from her. Furthermore he was in very bad health from eating too much; he fell
into a severe and incurable illness. The doctors call it dropsy: his
stomach was full of water and looked like a barrel; his legs were
swollen, his neck scrawny, his face thin, his thirst tremendous.
He looked like a lute; he stayed quietly in his house and was
treated by the physicians.[17] Pretending that it was a security
measure, but really in order to terrify others, the Tribune had
this deathly sick noble man seized in his own house, in the arms
of his wife, in his palace by the riverside, and had him led to the
Campidoglio. As soon as the robber baron had been conducted
to the Campidoglio, at about the ninth hour, the Tribune did not
waste a moment; he sounded the alarm bell; the people gathered;
Martino was stripped of his tasselled cloak, his hands were tied
behind his back, and he was made to kneel on the stairs beside
the Lion[18] in the usual place. There he heard his death sentence;
he was scarcely allowed enough time to confess himself perfectly
to the priest. He was condemned by the Tribune to be hanged
for having robbed the beached galley. This magnificent man was
led to the gallows on the esplanade of the Campidoglio and

16 In Ch. 16 of the complete chronicle, which described how a galley from
Marseilles ran aground on the seashore near Rome.
17 For a similar description of a dropsy victim (using the same image) see
Dante, *Inf.* xxx. 49-57.
18 An ancient statue of a lion, set up beside the stairs of the Palace; this
was where death sentences were pronounced.

there he was hanged; his wife, far off, could see him from the balconies of his house. One night and two days he hung on the gallows; his nobility did not help him, nor his kinship with the Orsini. Thus the Tribune ruled Rome, and many paid the ̖ penalty in the same way.

CHAPTER TWELVE

Because of the rigorous justice of the Tribune the aristocrats of Rome become so terrified that no further injustices occur, and even the Sultan of Babylon is frightened of him.

This event terrified the souls of the aristocrats, who were fully aware of their own evil activities ; some wept in commiseration, others were frightened. Now justice began to take vigor. The news of this deed terrified the magnates, who scarcely trusted themselves. Then the streets were open ; night and day travellers walked freely; no one dared to carry arms; no one injured others; masters dared not strike their servants; the Tribune watched over everything. Such an excellent deed made some weep for joy and pray that God would strengthen his heart and his mind. The Tribune's primary intention was to exterminate the tyrants and to confound them so thoroughly that no trace of them would be left. The carters who carried loads left them in the public streets; later they found them again safe and sound. Then a man named Tortora, one of the Tribune's couriers, was marked on the cheek because he had accepted money without permission, when he was sent to the Princes of Naples. The fame of so virtuous a man spread throughout the world; all Christendom was shaken as if wakened from sleep.

There was a Bolognese who had been a slave of the Sultan of Babylon. As soon as he could gain his freedom, he hastened to

Rome as quickly as possible. He said that the great Peraham had been told that in the city of Rome there had arisen a man of great justice, a man of the people; he answered, fearing for himself, and said, "Mahomet and holy Elinason help Jerusalem," by which he meant the land of the Saracens.

CHAPTER THIRTEEN

How the Tribune led his procession through the city, and how he was received by the clergy of St. Peter's when he visited that church.

In those days, after Martino was hanged, there was a festival of St. John in June; all Rome came to St. John in the morning. The Tribune wished to go to the festival like the others. This was how he went: he rode, with a great company of knights, mounted on a white war horse, dressed in white vestments lined with silk and decorated with gold laces. He looked beautiful and terrifying at the same time; the hundred sworn infantrymen of the region of Regola marched before him as he rode. A banner was carried above his head.

On another day, after dinner, he rode to St. Peter's of Rome; men and women ran to see him. This was the order of his beautiful procession: first came a militia of armed horsemen, handsomely adorned, who later were to march against the Prefect.[19] They were followed by the officials, judges, notaries, chamberlains, chancellors, Senate scribes, and all the officials, Peacemakers, and syndics. Then followed four marshals with their customary mounted escort, and then, following these, Janni

19 Cola's quarrel with Janni de Vico, hereditary Prefect of Rome, is described in Chs. 15 and 16 below.

de Allo, who carried a goblet of gilded silver in his hand with the offering that the Tribune was to make, as is done for a Senator. After him came the horse soldiers and after them the trumpeters playing silver trumpets. The crashing silver cymbals made a noble and magnificent sound. Then came the town criers; all these people passed by in silence. After these came a single man who carried in his hand a naked sword, as a sign of justice; he was Buccio, son of Jubileo. After him followed a man who went through all the streets throwing and scattering money, as is done in the Emperor's processions. Liello Migliaro was his name; on either side of him there were two men who carried sacks of money. After these the Tribune followed alone. He rode a great war horse, and was dressed in fur-lined silk, half green and half yellow. In his right hand he carried a brightly polished steel rod; on its summit was an apple of gilded silver, and above the apple a little cross of gold, which contained wood from the True Cross; and on one side letters were enameled which read DEVS, and on the other SPIRITVS SANCTVS. Directly after him came Cecco d'Alesso, who carried a standard above his head, as is done for a king. The field of this standard was white, with a sun of shining gold in the middle, surrounded by silver stars. On top of the standard was a white dove of silver which carried an olive crown in its beak. On his right and left marched fifty vassals of Vitorchiano, the True Men with pikes in hand; they looked very much like bears, dressed and armed.[20] After them followed the company of civilians: rich men, aristocrats, councillors, allies, and many other notable people. With such a triumph, with such glory he crossed the bridge of St. Peter, while everyone waved. The gates and barricades had been

---

20 In 1233 the town of Vitorchiano was made a vassal of Rome; from that time on its soldiers were known to the Romans as the "True Men."

demolished; the streets were clear and free.[21] After he arrived at the steps of St. Peter's, the Canons and all the clergy came out to meet him, solemnly dressed and prepared with white surplices, with the cross and incense; they came as far as the stairs singing VENI CREATOR SPIRITVS and received him with great rejoicing. Kneeling before the altar he made his offering; the clergy entrusted the possessions of St. Peter's to his care.

CHAPTER FOURTEEN

The Tribune continues to exercise his justice, punishing criminals ; he builds a palisade around the Palace of the Campidoglio, using all the fortifications of the barons of Rome, and forcing them and the former Senators to contribute to the repair of the Palace of the Campidoglio.

The following day the Tribune gave audience to the widows, orphans, and paupers; and he had two Senate scribes arrested and mitered[22] as forgers and charged them a large fine, a thousand pounds each. One was named Tomao Fortifiocca, the other Poncelletto della Cammora ; they were both very powerful plebeians. At first Cola led a very temperate life ; later he began to devote himself to feasts and banquets and debauches, with diverse foods and wines and elaborate confections. Next he had the Palace of the Campidoglio fenced in with a palisade between the columns, and closed it with timbers, and commanded that all the palisades belonging to the Roman barons be torn down, and

21 Many streets in Rome were commonly barricaded as a result of the barons' quarrels.

22 That is, crowned with a paper fool's cap (a "miter") on which the accusations against them were written; this common punishment for forgers is described in greater detail at the conclusion of Ch. 38 below.

it was done. He commanded that those beams and planks and timbers be carried to the Campidoglio at the barons' expense, and it was done. In the house of Messer Stefano della Colonna he then caught robbers whom he hanged. Then he fined each Senator one hundred florins; with this money he planned to rebuild and restore the Palace of the Campidoglio. He received a hundred florins from each baron, but the Palace was not rebuilt, though the work was begun. And he had Pietro de Agapito, who had been Senator that year, arrested, and he had his marshals lead him to court on foot, as if he were a robber. Now countless embassies from cities and from the nobles began to arrive. All Tuscany had already sent ambassadors.

CHAPTER FIFTEEN

The Tribune organizes a militia of infantrymen and cavalrymen, and afterwards summons the aristocrats to render obedience and pay the hearth tax. All obey except Janni di Vico, Tyrant of Viterbo, who however is deprived of his office by Cola.

Then the Tribune established the Militia of the Knights of Rome as follows: for each region of Rome he organized one hundred twenty infantrymen and thirty cavalrymen, and gave them pay; each cavalryman had a war horse and a pack horse, trappings for his horses, and new, decorated armor. They looked very much like barons. Then he organized the infantrymen, and equipped them well, and gave them banners bearing the arms of their regions, and gave them pay, and commanded them to be ready whenever the bell sounded, and made them swear fealty. There were one thousand three hundred infantrymen and three hundred sixty cavalrymen, select young men, skilled in warfare, and well armed.

Now that the Tribune was armed with the Militia he had thus created, he prepared to make war against more powerful people. He sent his edict around, and summoned all the aristocrats who lived within the territory of Rome. Meanwhile he appointed stewards and sent them to collect the hearth tax. So they gathered the ancient census of the people of Rome, and every day so much money came to Rome that it was hard work just to count it. The vassals of the barons quickly paid one carlin each for hearth tax. The cities, towns, and communes of lower Tuscany and Campagna and Marittima prepared to pay this tax. You would not have believed it: even the vassals of Antiochia paid. After he had sent the edict around to all the barons and to the cities, they obeyed graciously, as was said above; they paid humble reverence to Rome, their mother and lady. Only Janni de Vico, Prefect, Tyrant of Viterbo, would not submit; though summoned a thousand times, he refused to appear. So the Tribune passed sentence against the Prefect, and in public parliament deprived him of his office, and said that he was a fratricide and a rebel, and that he refused to return what was not his, that is, the Fortress of Rispampani; in this speech the Tribune called Janni de Vico by his name alone, without any titles.

CHAPTER SIXTEEN

The Tribune decides to go to war against Janni di Vico; he names Cola Orsino his captain, who besieges and captures the city of Vetralla. But Janni, hearing that the Tribune is planning to come in person, submits, and surrenders the Fortress of Rispampani, and is reinstated in his Prefecture.

Then the Tribune decided to go to war against the Prefect ; he made Cola Orsino, a squire and lord of Castel Sant'Angelo, his captain, and made Jordano delli Orzini his adviser. The army, strengthened by many allies, made camp above the city of Vetralla; they besieged it for sixty days, and swept over the whole plain as far as Viterbo, burning and pillaging. Lord, how they frightened the Viterbese! And so the inhabitants of Vetralla surrendered the city of their own free will. But it had a strong citadel, which was not surrendered. The Romans, wishing to capture it by the art of war, built slings and catapults. They threw a great many stones. Then they made a siege machine and brought it up as far as the gate of the citadel. That night the defenders of the citadel busied themselves and mixed up sulphur, pitch, oil, wood, turpentine, and other things, and threw this mixture on top of the machine. It caught fire that night; the next morning it was found in ashes.

In this army there were Cornetans with their troops and Manfredo, their lord. The garrisons of Perugia, Todi, and Narni, and many Roman barons were there. It was a beautiful, powerful, and noble army. By the time the Romans had destroyed every field, and had burnt the farms and the flax crop as far as Viterbo, it was mid-July and terribly hot. Then the Tribune determined to join the army in person, and to muster all his forces, cavalry and infantry, and destroy the vineyards of Viterbo. When the Prefect heard this he immediately decided to submit. At this time certain barons were imprisoned in the Campidoglio; they were not allowed to leave; they were Stefano della Colonna and Messer Jordano de Marini. First the Prefect sent ambassadors and then came to Rome in person. It was the ninth hour; at midday he entered the Campidoglio and submitted to the Tribune. He had about sixty men in his company. The gates of the Campidoglio were barred, the bell was sounded, and the men and women of Rome gathered. The Tribune held a parliament and said that Janni de Vico wished to submit to the people of Rome. Then he reinstated him in his Prefecture, saying that he was restoring the people's property. And so it happened, because before the Prefect left Rome, and before the army of Vetralla returned, the Fortress of Rispampani was opened to the stewards and syndic of Rome. And then the Prefect was released.

CHAPTER SEVENTEEN

How the Tribune had foreseen all this in a dream.

Now listen to news about dreams. The night before the day of the accord with the Prefect, the Tribune was sleeping in his splendid and triumphal bed. Soon after he fell asleep, he began to cry out loudly, saying, "Let me go, let me go!" At this the servants of the chamber ran up and said, "Sir, what is it? Do you want something?" Then the Tribune woke up and said, "Just now, just now I dreamt that a white friar came to me and said, 'Take your Fortress of Rispampani; look! I give it to you,' and saying this he took me by the hand while I slept. Then I cried out."

This dream turned out to be precisely true. There was a friar, named Fra Acuto, of the Hospitallers of Assisi, who founded the Hospital of the Cross of Santa Maria Rotunda, whom I mentioned above in my account of the rebuilding of Ponte Molle;[23] he was a good and holy person. This man negotiated the accord between the Romans and the Prefect. He came the following day to the Tribune with news of the peace, and said, "Take the Fortress of Rispampani; I give it to you." The Tribune was speaking to the people in parliament. The whole market street was filled; at the end of the street Fra Acuto appeared, dressed in white, mounted on his donkey, decked in white, crowned with olive

23 In Ch. 10 of the complete chronicle.

branches, with olive branches in his hand. Many people flocked to see him. From afar off the Tribune saw him and said to the servants of his bedchamber, "Look! last night's dream." In the army of Vetralla the Romans had one thousand cavalrymen and six thousand infantrymen; the army returned to Rome crowned with olive branches.

CHAPTER EIGHTEEN

A discussion about dreams, which sometimes turn out true, like those of Fra Merulus, the Emperor Marcian, and Cassius.

At this point I wish to digress a little from my material. Someone may ask if dreams can be true. To this I answer that although many are meaningless and many are diabolical delusions, nevertheless many do turn out to be true, just as if inspired by God, especially in temperate persons who have not clouded their minds with debauchery and strange foods, and especially at the time of night called aurora, when night is becoming day, when the brain is purified, and the spirits temperate.

The blessed St. Gregory bears witness to this in his *Dialogue*,[24] where he says that in his monastery there lived a holy and virtuous monk named Merulus. Chief among Merulus' many virtues was this: he never stopped reciting the Psalms, except while he was eating or sleeping. He became sick; while sleeping he dreamt that a beautiful crown of various flowers came down from heaven and was placed on his head. He told the other monks about this dream; he then died, and, since he believed that his dream was a good sign, he passed on joyfully.

24 Gregory the Great, *Dial.* 4.49 (paraphrased).

Fourteen years after his death another monk dug a grave for a dead man in the place where Merulus was buried. When the grave was dug, suddenly a fragrance arose from that place, a sweet odor, as if there were roses, violets, lilies, and many other flowers in the trench. And so Merulus' dream, that a crown of flowers had come to him from heaven, turned out to be very true, since the flowers could send out an odor from the grave fourteen years later.

Furthermore Fra Martinus mentions this subject in his *Chronicle*.[25] He says that the Emperor Marcian, while in Constantinople, dreamt one night that he saw the arch of Attila broken in two. Marcian judged that this meant that Attila was dead, and this turned out to be true. This Attila was a great king and a great tyrant. He had many archers in his army; he went through all Pannonia and Bulgaria spreading ruin; he destroyed many cities, Aquileia among them; he killed his brother Bleda; and finally he was defeated by the French, Burgundians, Saxons, and Italians. In that battle the King of Burgundy died, along with a hundred eighty thousand men, so that a river of blood flowed. And so King Attila, since he was defeated, returned to his country and gathered a huge number of Hungarians and Dacians, and returned to invade Italy again. One of the first towns he came across was Aquileia, which he destroyed. The most holy Pope Leo was living at that time; he begged Attila to leave Italy, and so it happened. When Attila left Italy to return to his own land, he died in Pannonia. On the night of his death the Emperor Marcian, at Constantinople in Greece, dreamt that he saw the arch of Attila broken; therefore he guessed that Attila was dead, and so it happened.

25 Martinus Polonus, *Chronicon* s.v. *Valens* (*MGH* SS. XXII 454; paraphrased).

Furthermore Valerius Maximus[26] mentions the dream of Cassius Parmensis, who had killed Julius Caesar and had therefore fled Rome. Octavian and Antony pursued him as a mortal enemy. One night this Cassius withdrew into a little fortress. Having gone to bed, he saw in a dream a terrible man with a dark face who threatened him. His threats were in the Greek language. Twice he awoke from his dream; the third time he had a light brought in and commanded his servants to guard him. He also saw the same dream the next day. This dream was well verified because the legions of Octavian and the army of Antony overcame him, and Cassius was captured and his head was cut off.

CHAPTER NINETEEN

On the opinion of Aristotle concerning the causes and variety of dreams.

The philosopher Aristotle mentions this and deals with it in detail in his book, *On Sleep and Waking,* in the chapter on divination.[27] Aristotle and his followers say that a dream can be true naturally, and this he subtly demonstrates in the following way. First the Philosopher argues that the difference between waking and sleeping is that when we are awake large movements seem small to the imagination, while in sleep small movements and small objects seem large. Hence it happens that in one person a little sweet phlegm flows through the mouth and seems to him to taste of sugar, honey, and cinnamon; in another a little choler flows and it seems to him that arrows are flying through

26 Valerius Maximus 1.7.7 (paraphrased).
27 Aristotle, *Div. Somn.* 462b-464b (paraphrased).

the air, and fires, flames, and tempests; in another the wind
blows, or even a tiny breeze, and he thinks a storm is raging.
The reason for this is that in sleep all the spirits are brought
together within the fantasy and the imagination, and thus they
are more sensitive. Also, because they are gathered together,
they are more potent in their operation. When we are awake,
however, the spirits are dispersed, and there are many and
various objects; but when the power is united it is stronger than
when it is scattered. Now we know that in the night the spirits
are eager, intent, and easily moved. Aristotle's second presup-
position is this: he says that the air is what we work through;
without it we cannot live. Air is in the midst of us; the human
voice goes from man to man because the air is refracted from
man to man; the air is changed and moves according to the
changes which men make, just as happens with forms which are
reflected in a mirror. Take another example: someone throws a
rock in a lake; the rock moves the water; the part of the water
which has been moved moves the next part in a circular fashion,
and it continues to make circles as long as the force of the throw
lasts. A fisherman stands with his fish-hook; he fishes; he does
not see the man who threw the rock, but he sees the rings in the
water; he realizes that someone is making it hard for him to
catch fish; he gets up and goes to ask him not to throw any more
rocks. In the same way, says Aristotle, the human voice changes
the air; the air, changed from part to part, reaches the senses of
men and other animals, just as happens when fetid matter and
dead bodies throw corrupt vapors through the air, which reach
the sense of smell of wolves and vultures; in fact it is written
that vultures fly five hundred miles to dead bodies. This occurs
because of the changes which make the air continually corrupt
from body to body.

Now Aristotle maintains that the air is changed not only by
physical action, but also by the will. Let us now imagine a man

who wishes to kill another; the spirits within him are inflamed; the inflamed spirits change the air according to the quality of that kindled choler; the changed air reaches the intended victim. He is asleep, and therefore his spirits are attuned and sensitive; he senses the anger of his enemy, either in his own appearance or in something similar. This is the natural reason which the Philosopher adduces. Thus it is perfectly understandable that the Emperor saw the broken arch of Attila in a dream, since through the death of Attila the air in the atmosphere was changed, and moved directly from one place to another, and reached the spirit of the sleeping Emperor. Now I shall return to my material.

CHAPTER TWENTY

Many castles and fortresses are surrendered to the Tribune, and many aristocrats submit to him. He builds a chapel in his palace. Here he attends Mass, and his wife is courted by the noblewomen, and his relatives by the citizens.

After the Prefect submitted and handed over the Fortress of Rispampani, the strong and opulent Castle of Ceri in Marittima was immediately surrendered to the Tribune; then Monticelli near Tivoli, Vitorchiano near Viterbo, the Castle of Civitavecchia on the seashore, Piglio in Campagna, and Porto by the Tiber. He then had in his hands all the fortresses, passes, and bridges of Rome. Encouraged by this he named Janni Colonna his captain against any Campanians who might rebel, especially against the Count of Fondi, Janni Gaetano; and Janni and the Campanians submitted. The Prefect, to show his obedience, sent his son Francesco as a hostage, very honorably accompanied. Then Cola de Buccio de Braccia, an aristocrat who lived in the mountains of Rieti, fled as quickly as possible, far from the land of Rome.

Then the Tribune built a beautiful chapel in the Campidoglio, enclosed with tin-plated iron gratings. There he had solemn Mass sung with plenty of singers and many lights. Then he had all the barons of Rome stand before him while he was seated, right on their feet, with arms folded and hoods doffed. Lord, how frightened they were! This Cola had a very young and beautiful wife, who, when she went to St. Peter's, went accompanied by armed youths, followed by the noblewomen; serving-maids with subtle little feathers made a breeze before her face, and industriously fanned her, so that her face would not be offended by flies. He had an uncle named Janni Varvieri; he was a barber; he was made a great lord, and was called Janni Roscio; he went about on horseback well accompanied by Roman citizens. So it went with all his relatives: he had a widowed sister whom he planned to marry to an aristocrat.

CHAPTER TWENTY-ONE

From far-off cities and castles people come to Rome for justice which produces the best of effects. And Cola, wishing to be sole lord, dismisses the Pope's vicar and sends an embassy to His Holiness.

The Tribune named officials and renewed their prerogatives. Fame and terror of his excellent government spread into every land. From far-off cities and countries people came to Rome to make accusations; and you would scarcely believe how many made appeals and how many were punished. In the city of Perugia a rich Jewish moneylender and his wife were secretly killed. An inquiry into the murder was promptly held in Rome. Many victims of tyranny from the cities of Tuscany came to Rome and begged the Tribune in God's name to restore their homes to them. He promised to do his best for everyone.

Now foreigners came in droves; the inns were full because of the great crowd of foreigners; abandoned houses were repaired; the market thronged with people. The lords of Montagna, and those of Molieti, and Todino de Antonio, who had always been strangers to Rome, all appeared. Wishing to be sole lord in such a prosperous time, the Tribune dismissed his colleague, the Pope's vicar, who was a great ultramontane decretalist and Bishop of Viterbo, although he had many letters and many commissions from the great prelates at Avignon. Then he sent an ambassador to the Pope to report what had happened. When this ambassador returned he said that the Pope and all the cardinals had very serious doubts.

CHAPTER TWENTY-TWO

The principal cities and princes of Christendom send ambassadors to the Tribune.

Now I will tell you about the distinguished embassies which came to him. All Rome was joyous and smiling, and appeared to have returned to the better years of the past. The venerable and triumphal legation of the Florentines came to Rome, and that of the Sienese, and those of Arezzo, Todi, Terni, Spoleto, Rieti, Amelia, Tivoli, Velletri, Pistoia, Fuligno, and Assisi. These and many other respected men, persons of honorable position, sent embassies: judges, knights, merchants, beautiful and eloquent orators, and men of wisdom. All these cities and communes offered themselves to the Good Estate; the cities of Campagna, the Duchy, and the towns of the Patrimony delivered themselves to the Good Estate, rejecting the authority of the Church.[28] The

28 The "Duchy" is the Duchy of Spoleto; the "Patrimony" is the Patrimony of St. Peter (i.e., southern Tuscany).

people of Gaeta sent ten thousand florins with their embassy and offered themselves. The Venetians wrote letters sealed with the pendent lead seal in which they offered their persons and property to the Good Estate. Messer Luchino, the great Tyrant of Milan, sent a letter urging the Tribune to govern well, and warning him to rule the barons cautiously.

Most of the Tyrants of Lombardy ignored him: Messer Taddeo delli Pepoli of Bologna, the Marquis Obizzo of Ferrara, Messer Mastino della Scala of Verona, Messer Filippino da Gonzaga of Mantua, and the Signori De Carrara of Padua. In Romagna Messer Francesco delli Ordelaffi of Forlì, Messer Malatesta of Rimini, and many other tyrants first gave a filthy and insulting response, but then took more mature counsel and prepared to send him solemn embassies. Louis, Duke of Bavaria, the former Emperor, sent secret ambassadors all the way from Germany and prayed in God's name that the Tribune reconcile him with the Church, since he did not wish to die excommunicated.

From the Kingdom of Puglia the Duke of Durazzo wrote to him and offered himself, beginning his letter with the words, "To our dearest friend." Messer Louis, Prince of Taranto, and other princes wrote to him. From Louis, King of Hungary, came a great and honorable embassy. Now the ambassadors' prebends came and asked the Tribune and the people of Rome to avenge the cruel death of King Andrew of Puglia, who had been hanged by the barons, as will be explained later.[29] These prebends were two notable persons, dressed in rich green fur-lined cloth, with German cloaks. When the Tribune heard their embassy, he brought them onto the speaker's platform to answer them before all the people. It was Saturday; a trial had just been held. Then

29 In Ch. 19 (now lost) of the complete chronicle.

he had the tribunal crown, which I shall describe later,[30] placed on his head. In his right hand he held a silver apple with a cross, and said, "I shall judge the world in justice, and the people in equity."[31] Then he said, "These are the ambassadors of the Hungarians, who demand justice for the death of the innocent King Andrew." From Queen Joan, wife of the unfortunate King Andrew, he received gracious letters, and his wife received five hundred florins and jewels from her.

From the Holy Apostolic Father he received letters admonishing him to do well, and letters from many prelates urging him to suck the breasts of the Holy Church, his sweet and merciful Mother. Philip of Valois, King of France, sent a letter by an archer. It was written in the vernacular; it was not pompous, but like a merchant's letter. When the letter arrived in Rome, the Tribune had fallen from power; his government had collapsed; therefore the letter was given to the lords of Castel Sant'Angelo, and eventually it reached the hands of Agnilo Malabranca, Chancellor of Rome.

CHAPTER TWENTY-THREE

Concerning the magnificent responses which Cola gave to the ambassadors.

I want to describe briefly the magnificent responses he gave. The embassy of the Prince of Taranto came to Rome; there were three ambassadors, an Archbishop of the Franciscan order,

---

30 Perhaps a reference to Ch. 35 below; the description of the crown given there, however, is so perfunctory that it seems likely that a chapter describing the Tribune's coronation of 15 August has been lost.

31 Cf. *Ps.* 9:9: "And he shall judge the world in equity, he shall judge the people in justice" (Douay).

Master in Theology; a knight with golden spurs, and a judge, with a beautiful company, baggage and other household stuff. When the three ambassadors appeared before the Tribune, the Archbishop propounded these words: "He sent men to renew the amity." Then he spoke at length and told how happy his lord was with the new government of Rome; then he encouraged the Tribune; then he promised help; then he asked that the Romans unite against the King of Hungary, who was coming to burn and ravage the Kingdom of Puglia. With this the ambassador came to an end.

The Tribune, without any preparation, responded in the following way. First he propounded the words: "Far be the sword and arms from us; let there be peace by sea and by land." Then he said, "We have some plebeians whom we must consult before giving you an answer." When the friar who was Master in Theology heard these words, he was so frightened that he did not know what to say. He was afraid because the response of the Tribune answered to his proposition, and both of them were from one text, a short distance from each other, in the Book of the Maccabees.[32] This is how the story goes; a foreign nation invaded the Kingdom of Judaea. The princes of Judaea resisted stoutly; the war was great; the fields were not cultivated; there was great famine throughout the land, they had no forage. It happened that the Jews looked to the Romans, with whom they had a treaty, for assistance; they sent ambassadors to Rome to renew this alliance and ask for aid and succor. They also came to ask for grain because of the famine; for this they brought

32 The Archbishop's statement is based on 1 *Mac.* 12:1: "And Jonathan saw that the time served him, and he chose certain men, and sent them to Rome, to confirm and to renew the amity with them" (Douay). Cola's reply is based on 1 *Mac.* 8:23: "Good success be to the Romans, and to the people of the Jews, by sea, and by land, for ever; and far be the sword and enemy from them" (Douay).

ships and plenty of money. The Romans answered in a letter, writing that they prayed that there would be no war in the land of Judaea, and that God would grant them peace by land and sea. At the grain supply station the Romans loaded the ships with grain, and put the money in sacks; and the grain was sent, and the money returned. Of this the friar was afraid; he thought to himself, "This Tribune is a very wise and learned man; he answered me through the text of the Bible, in the same column where our proposition stood. Certainly he knows much; he is shrewd and erudite."

CHAPTER TWENTY-FOUR

Notable examples of the good justice of the Tribune.

Now I want to tell you something about the justice which this man administered. I confess that those who sell meat and fish in Rome are the worst men in the world; they cheat all sorts of people. But now they said clearly: this meat is from a sheep, this is from a goat, this is no longer fresh; this fish is good, this is bad. Each guild simply told the truth.

Among the other ambassadors a black friar from Città di Castello came to Rome; he stayed at an inn in the Campo de' Fiori. In the evening when he got up from dinner he could not find his cloak, which he had left outside; it had been stolen. The monk had some words with the innkeeper. The innkeeper said, "You didn't consign your cloak to me." Not wishing to trouble the innkeeper any further about finding the cloak, the monk went to the Tribune and said, "Sir, I was eating dinner and left my cloak outside the inn; I believed that your government would keep it safe for me. Now it has been stolen from me; I can't replace it. I am a consecrated monk; I am dressed only in this gown; I travel light, like a sparrow hawk." To this the Tribune answered, "Your cloak is safe." He sent for cloth, and then and there he had a rich cloak of the same cloth and color cut and sewn for him. Now the monk returned very happily to the inn and said, "I didn't lose anything; look: my cloak." The Tribune's notary made a record of where the theft had taken place, and if the Tribune had not fallen from power so soon he would have exacted a fine of more than one thousand florins for the theft.

In the district of the Castle of Capranica a carter was robbed; a mule was taken from him, and a load of oil. For good faith Count Vertuollo, who was lord of the Castle, sent thirty florins for the oil and the mule, and he paid four hundred florins fine for guarding the country badly.

A courier was carrying letters for the Tribune; while he was sleeping at his inn at night, another courier killed him and took his money. The criminal was caught and buried alive, and the corpse of the murdered man was placed over him in the grave.

Also the more noble question of the death of King Andrew was dealt with in Rome. The lawyers for the King of Hungary and the lawyers for Queen Joan appeared before the bench of the Tribune's judge and put their questions. The lawyers of the King demanded justice; those of the Queen said that she was innocent of the death of her husband. The other side complained of the injury and kept demanding vengeance. The arguments of one side and the other were put in a book. This was a great and honorable event.

CHAPTER TWENTY-FIVE

The Tribune takes the Order of Knighthood with great pomp and ceremony.

Now I want to tell you how the Tribune was made a knight. After he saw that everything was going well and that he was ruling peacefully without opposition, he began to desire the honor of knighthood. And so he was made a knight of the bath on the vigil of the Assumption in August.[33] This grand festival was arranged in the following way. First the Tribune prepared the whole Lateran Palace and the surrounding area for the investiture; for days before he had dining tables built from the timbers and beams of the stockades of the barons of Rome ; these tables were placed throughout the old hall of the old Palace; everyone who looked at them was astonished. The walls of the hall were broken open and wooden stairways leading to the courtyard were built to allow the food, which was to be cooked outdoors, to be brought in; and for each hall he prepared a supply of wine in the corner. It was the vigil of St. Peter in Chains, at the ninth hour. All Rome, men and women, went to St. John's; people stood on the porticoes to see the festival, and on the public streets to see this triumph.

First knights from many nations passed by: barons, plebeians, and foreigners with bells on their horses' harnesses; they were dressed in silk, with banners; they made merry; they ran and played. Then countless musicians followed, playing trumpets, bagpipes, cymbals, and harps. After them came the Tribune's wife, who walked with her mother. Many well-born ladies accompanied them because they wanted to please them. Before her went two elegantly dressed young men, carrying a noble golden bridle in their hands. Then came trumpeters playing countless silver trumpets. After these came a great number of equestrian players, of whom the Perugians and Cornetans were the most skilful. Twice they threw their vestments of silk into the crowd.

33 The Chronicler has confused two ceremonies: Cola's assumption of knighthood (here described) took place on 1 August 1347 (the Feast of St. Peter in Chains), his coronation (not described by the Chronicler) on 15 August (the Feast of the Assumption).

Then came the Tribune, and the Pope's vicar beside him. Before the Tribune came a man who carried in his hand a naked sword; above his head another carried a banner, while in his own hand he was carrying a staff of steel. Many notable people were in his company. He was dressed in a white silk robe, astonishingly bright, decorated with threads of gold.

In the evening at twilight he went up to the Chapel of Pope Boniface and spoke to the people, saying, "You know that this evening I am to be made a knight. Return tomorrow, and you will hear things which will delight God in heaven and men on earth." Everywhere in the great multitude there was joy; there was no disturbance or fighting. Two men had angry words and drew their swords; before striking a blow they returned them to their sheaths, and everyone went on his way. The inhabitants of the neighboring cities came to this festival. What more? the old men and the young girls, the widows and the matrons.

After all the people had departed, the clergy celebrated a solemn Office, and then the Tribune entered the Baptistry and bathed in the basin of the Emperor Constantine, which is made of the most precious touchstone.[34] This was an amazing deed, and it gave rise to a good deal of talk. A citizen of Rome, Messer Vico Scuotto, Knight, bound on his sword. Afterwards he slept in an honorable bed, there in the Baptistry of St. John, within the circuit of the columns. There he spent the whole night. Now see a marvel: the bed and the bedstead were new; when the Tribune came to get into bed, one part of the bed suddenly fell to the ground, and thus it remained through the silent night.

When morning came the Tribune rose and dressed in scarlet trimmed with fur; his sword was bound on by Messer Vico

34 According to tradition Pope Sylvester had cleansed the Emperor Constantine of leprosy by bathing him in this basin. Cola's bath was a normal part of the ceremony of knighthood, but his use of this basin was considered sacrilegious by his critics.

Scuotto, along with spurs of gold as a sign of knighthood. All Rome and all the knights went from there to St. John's; the barons and foreigners and citizens gathered to see Messer Cola de Rienzi, Knight. There was great festivity and great rejoicing.

CHAPTER TWENTY-SIX

The Tribune, having been made a knight, publicly summons the Pope, the College of Cardinals, the Bavarian, and the Imperial Electors, and performs other acts of jurisdiction.

Messer Nicola stood adorned as a knight in the Chapel of Boniface above the piazza with a solemn company. There a solemn Mass was sung, with plenty of singers and elaborate decorations. During this ceremony the Tribune appeared before the people and said in a loud voice, "We summon Pope Clement to come to his diocese in Rome." Then he summoned the College of Cardinals, and the Bavarian,[35] and the Imperial Electors of Germany, saying, "I want these men to come to Rome; I want to see if they have the right to elect the Emperor." He said that he had found it written that after the lapse of a certain amount of time the election fell to the Romans. After this summons was proclaimed, letters were prepared at once, and couriers, and they were sent on their way. Then the Tribune drew his sword from its sheath and waved it in the air toward the three divisions of the world, saying, "This is mine; this is mine; this is mine."[36]

35 That is, Louis of Bavaria, the deposed Holy Roman Emperor.
36 This action, which is apt to strike a modern observer as proof of megalomaniacal insanity, is actually no more than a slight exaggeration of a normal part of the imperial coronation ceremony.

The Pope's vicar was present while all this was going on; he stood there like a block of wood. He was stunned and dumbfounded, but nevertheless he protested. He summoned one of his notaries and prepared a public announcement stating that these things were being done against his will, without his knowledge, and without the Pope's permission. And he asked the notary to draw up a public document. While the notary, crying out in a high voice, made these protests to the people, Messer Nicola commanded that the trumpets, kettledrums, and cymbals be played, so that the noise would keep the notary's voice from being heard. The greater sound concealed the smaller: a wicked piece of clownery. After this the Mass and its solemnity were completed.

Listen to a notable thing. All through that day, from dawn till the ninth hour, the bronze horse of Constantine,[37] through specially placed lead pipes, poured out a stream of red wine through its right nostril and water through its left, which fell ceaselessly into a brimming basin. All the youth, citizens and strangers, who were thirsty gathered around there and drank and made merry.

CHAPTER TWENTY-SEVEN

After the ceremony of knighthood the Tribune holds a solemn banquet, and then returns to the Campidoglio.

After it became known that the Tribune had bathed in the basin of Constantine, and that he had summoned the Pope, people were very suspicious and dubious about it. Some rebuked him for audacity; some said that he was a fantastic madman.

37 The bronze equestrian statue of Marcus Aurelius, which now stands in the piazza of the Campidoglio. The mediaeval belief that it represented Constantine, the first Christian emperor, saved it from destruction.

Now they went to the most solemn banquet of elaborate foods and noble wines; many lords and ladies were present. Messer Nicola and the Pope's vicar sat alone at the marble table, the pontifical table. It was in the old hall of St. John's. The whole hall was full of tables. His wife ate with the ladies in the hall of the new Papal Palace. At this banquet water was scarcer than wine. Anyone who wished to was free to come to the banquet. There was no order there: abbots, clergy, knights, merchants, and other people all sat together. There were many confections of various types; there was an abundance of sturgeon, delicate fish, pheasant, and kid. Whoever wanted to take home the leftovers could do so freely. The ambassadors who had come from various countries were at this banquet. Among the many entertainers at the feast was one dressed in an ox skin; he had horns on his head; he looked like an ox; he played and leapt. When the banquet was finished, Messer Nicola de Rienzi, dressed in scarlet trimmed with fur, returned to the Campidoglio with a large mounted escort.

I do not want to omit the things he had made for himself during his ascendancy. He made a box with a hole on top, once very valuable, though worthless later. He also made a hat all of pearls, very beautiful, with a dove of pearls on top. These various vices led to his downfall and brought him to perdition.

CHAPTER TWENTY-EIGHT

The Tribune under various pretexts has the barons come to him, and then imprisons them.

One day the Tribune invited Messer Stefano della Colonna the Elder, who was spoken of above,[38] to dinner. When it was

38 In Ch. 7 of this Book and Ch. 2 of the complete chronicle. The Stefano della Colonna described in Chs. 33-35 below is Stefano the Elder's son.

dinner time, he had him seized and brought into the Campidoglio, and there he held him. Then he arrested Pietro de Agabito,
Lord of Genazzano, who was Provost of Marseilles, and Senator
of Rome that year, and Lubertiello, son of Count Vertuollo, who
was also Senator. He had these two Senators brought to the
Campidoglio also, as if they were criminals. He also arrested the
gallant young Janni Colonna, whom he had made captain over
Campagna a few days earlier. He arrested Jordano delli Orzini
dello Monte, Messer Ranallo delli Orzini de Marini, Cola Urzino, Lord of the Castel Sant'Angelo; Count Vertuollo, Messer
Orzo de Vicovaro delli Orzini, and many other great barons of
Rome. He could not capture Luca de Saviello, Stefano della
Colonna, or Messer Jordano de Marini. The Tribune held the
above-mentioned barons in prison under guard; he captured
them by a sort of betrayal, inviting some of them to come and
consult with him, and others to dine.

When evening came, the Roman plebeians who were there
denounced the evil of the nobles and praised the excellence of
the Tribune. Then Messer Stefano the Elder put a question, to
wit: if it was proper for a leader of the people to be prodigal or
avaricious. There was much dispute over this. After all the
others had spoken, Messer Stefano, taking the hem of the
Tribune's noble robe, said, "For you, Tribune, it would be more
commendable to wear the plain clothes of a poor man than these
pompous garments." And saying this he held up the hem of the
robe. When he heard this, Cola de Rienzi was troubled. That
evening he had all the nobles imprisoned and set guards over
them. Messer Stefano the Elder was shut up in the hall where
audiences are held. All night long, without any bed to sleep in,
he paced back and forth, pounding on the door and begging the
guards to open. The guards did not listen to him. A cruel thing
was done to him through all that pitiless night.

CHAPTER TWENTY-NINE

The Tribune has the death sentence announced to the imprisoned barons, but, allowing himself to be persuaded by the advice of some citizens, he frees them, giving them titles and gifts.

Now it was day. The Tribune had made up his mind to execute all of them in public in order to free the Roman people from them once and for all. He commanded that the audience hall be decorated with red and white silk bunting, and it was done. This he did to symbolize blood. Then he had the bell rung, and the people gathered. Then he sent a Minorite as confessor to all the barons, so that they could do penance and take the Body of Christ. When the barons heard this and heard the alarm bell ringing, they became so petrified that they could not speak; they did not know what to do. Most of them humbled themselves and did penance and took communion. Messer Ranallo delli Orsini and another man, because they had eaten fresh figs early in the morning, could not take communion. Messer Stefano della Colonna refused to confess or take communion. He said that he was not ready and had not yet arranged his affairs.

Meanwhile some Roman citizens, weighing carefully the judgment which the Tribune planned to make, restrained him with sweet and flattering words. Finally they changed his mind, and he gave up his proposal. It was the hour of tierce; all the barons went down as condemned men to the audience hall. Trumpets were sounded, as if the barons were going to be executed. They stood before the people. The Tribune, having changed his plan, ascended the platform and delivered a beautiful speech. It was based on the words of the Lord's prayer: forgive us our trespasses. Then he pardoned the barons, saying that they were willing to serve the people and be reconciled with them. One by one they bowed their heads to the people. He made some of them patricians and others prefects of the grain supply; one he made Duke of Tuscany, another Duke of Campagna. He gave them each a beautiful robe trimmed with fur and a banner decorated with golden ears of grain. Then he had them dine with him, and rode about with them through Rome. Then he let them go their ways.[39]

Discreet men were very displeased with this deed. The people said, "This man has lit a fire and flame which he will not be able to put out. And I would remind him of the proverb which says that a man ought to shit or get off the pot."

CHAPTER THIRTY

The liberated barons plot against Cola, fortifying Marino and other strongholds, whence they are summoned by the Tribune. But instead of obeying they make forays as far as the gates of Rome.

Now I will tell you how the castle of Marino was besieged. After the barons were released they did not gather their forces; they left Rome and went to their fortresses, muttering threats between their teeth. None of them dared attack the Romans. Meanwhile the Colonna and the Lords of Marino, Messer Ranallo and Messer Jordano, fortified their castles and plotted in secret. It was clear that they planned to rebel. They fortified Marino, renovated the moat, and put a strong palisade of double wood around it. The Tribune was so mad that he did not know enough to forbid this. He did not prepare himself from the start; he waited until the castle was all rigged out. Meanwhile many

39 Cola described this event in a letter (*Epistolario* 23) to Rinaldo Orsini, papal notary at Avignon, in which he denies that he ever intended to execute the barons; the confessors, he says, mistakenly told the barons that this was his intention.

people began to murmur about the Tribune's wickedness. After the castle of Marino was well fortified, and supplied with arrows, lances, men, provisions, walls, timbers, and wine, the rebellion was discovered. An edict was issued demanding that the rebels return to Rome. The messenger was wounded in the head no less than three times, there among the vineyards of Marino. Then they made forays from Marino, and plundered the fields of Rome every day. They carried off cattle, sheep, pigs, and beasts of burden, and took them all to Marino. Now there was tearing of cheeks in Rome; every person shrieked his complaint; rancor and fear arose.

A second time the Tribune summoned them and commanded that they come to Rome under penalty of his wrath. He ordered a picture of Messer Ranallo and Messer Jordano, portraying them as knights turned upside down, to be painted in front of the Palace of the Campidoglio. In retaliation Messer Jordano did worse than ever. He made a raid as far as the Porta San Giovanni and captured men, women, and beasts of burden, and took everything to Marino. His brother, Messer Ranallo, crossed the Tiber and entered the city of Nepi, and made raids on this side and that, burning and looting. He burnt the towns, the castle, houses, and people. He did not hesitate to burn a noble lady, a widow, inside a tower. This cruelty infuriated the Romans; they became enraged at Messer Ranallo and Messer Jordano. It did not seem a joking matter; the perverse mind of the Romans turned against the Colonna.

CHAPTER THIRTY-ONE

The Tribune goes to Marino with an army, captures the Castelluza, and does much damage; summoned again and again from there by the Pope's Legate, he returns to Rome.

It was then the time of vintage; the grapes were ripe; the people were trampling them. The Tribune gathered all his soldiers and led his army out of Rome. He marched against the castle of Marino and encamped in a place called Macchantrevola; it is a valley under a long forest, about a mile from the castle. The army was beautiful, strong, and well equipped with infantrymen and cavalrymen. There were twenty thousand infantrymen and eight hundred cavalrymen. The weather was so angry and wet that it impeded the army. It did not allow them to do any plundering. Finally, after about eight days, they devastated the land around the castle of Marino; they depopulated the whole area; they cut down vines and trees ; they burnt mills; they levelled the noble forest which up to that time had been untouched; they destroyed everything. For years afterward that castle was not so strong nor so great. Then they took all the loot they could from the treasuries. All Rome was there.

In those days a Cardinal,[40] a papal legate, came unexpectedly to Rome. This Legate kept pestering the Tribune with letters urging him to return to Rome to discuss something with him. The Tribune, after the devastation was finished, broke camp early one morning and marched against the Castelluza, a short distance from Marino. He captured it at once, and the walls around it were immediately levelled. Now he planned to attack the citadel and the round tower where the infantry had retreated; to take the tower by storm he had two wooden castles built, which rolled on wheels, and were equipped with ladders and wooden towers. You have never seen such clever devices. He prepared pikes and other instruments. He received many embassies there. In a rivulet which ran there he christened two dogs, naming them Ranallo and Jordano, dog knights. Then he destroyed the Mill, and finally he returned to Rome with his army, because the Legate's letters were urging him to come back.

40 Cardinal Bertrand de Déaux.

Early in the morning he tore down the beautiful palaces at the foot of St. Peter's Bridge in front of San Celso.[41] Then he went with his knights to St. Peter's, entered the sacristy, and put the imperial state Dalmatic on over his armor. The emperors wore this Dalmatic at their coronations; it is a rich garment, all decorated with little pearls. Wearing this garment over his armor like a Caesar, he entered the Papal Palace, with trumpets sounding, and appeared before the Legate, his scepter in his hand, his crown on his head. He looked terrible and fantastic. When he had come before the Legate, the Tribune spoke, saying, "You have sent for us: what is it your pleasure to command?" The Legate replied, "We have many instructions from our Lord the Pope." When the Tribune heard this, he raised his voice and shouted, "What instructions are these?" When the Legate heard this biting answer, he restrained himself and kept silent. The Tribune turned and left, and made war against the Marinans: the Marinans against the Romans.

CHAPTER THIRTY-TWO

The Colonna take up arms in Palestrina and march against Rome, with many other barons. The Tribune takes up arms, and, suspicious of the Prefect, who had come to help him, he puts him in prison.

Now I will tell you how the Colonna were defeated in Rome. The war was hard; the citizens of Rome were worn out by the hard work, discomfort, and destruction; the Tribune did not pay the soldiers as he used to; there was great muttering through the

41 These were the Orsini palaces. Cola is here breaking his own law; see above, Ch. 6, third ordinance.

city. The plebeian knights of Rome sent letters to Messer Stefano della Colonna, asking him to come with soldiers: they wanted to open the gates for him. The Colonna held a muster in Palestrina; they numbered about seven hundred cavalrymen and four thousand infantrymen. They planned to force their way into Rome. Many barons were in on the plot with them. Great preparations were made in Palestrina; in order to get into Rome they sent out sweet messages, saying that they only wanted to return to their homes. The Tribune was terribly frightened by this muster, and began to behave like a sick madman; he neither ate nor slept.

Early one morning, about three days before the battle, the Tribune spoke to the people and encouraged them; among other things he said, "I want you to know that last night St. Martin, who was a tribune's son, appeared to me and said, 'Do not doubt that you will kill the enemies of God.'" Early the following morning, before dawn, he sounded the alarm bell, gathered the people all in arms, and in a well-ordered speech said, "Gentlemen, I want to tell you that tonight the holy Pope Boniface[42] appeared to me and said that on this very day we shall take vengeance on his enemies the Colonna, who disgraced the Church of God so foully." He added, "I have a son named Lorienzo who will join me in the battle against the betrayers of the people, and against the perjurers." Then he said, "We know from our spies that these people have come and made camp four miles from the city in a place called the Monument. And this is a true sign that not only will they be defeated, but they will also be killed and buried in that Monument." After saying this, he had the trumpets, cymbals, and kettledrums sounded, and set out the troops and appointed captains, and gave the watchword,

42 Pope Boniface VIII, who had been seized and insulted by Sciarra della Colonna in 1303.

"Knights of the Holy Ghost." When this was done, calmly, noiselessly, with the legions of infantry and cavalry in order, they went to the gate of San Lorenzo, known as the Porta Tiburtina. Barons who were there with the people included Jordano delli Orzini, Cola Orzino of the Castel Sant' Angelo, Malabranca della Pescina, the Chancellor; his son Mattheo, Lubertiello son of Count Vertuollo, and many others.

I do not want to omit the way the Tribune treated the Prefect before the battle. The Tribune sent for the Prefect. The Prefect, wishing to obey, came with one hundred cavalrymen to take part in the battle on the side of the Romans. He brought with him around fifteen lesser nobles of Tuscany. He also brought his son Francesco, who was carrying arms for the first time. He sent five hundred loads of grain for provisions, as a Prefect ought to do. He had been forced to please the Romans. When he arrived, he was invited to dinner; while he was sitting there his arms were taken from him and from his company, and he and his son were imprisoned; their weapons and horses were given to the Romans. And the Tribune held a meeting with the people, in which he said, "Do not be amazed that I am holding the Prefect in prison; he came here to stab the Roman people in the back and to destroy them."

CHAPTER THIRTY-THREE

The Colonna arrive at Rome with their army and find the gates barred. But while the army is passing in procession the gate is opened; Janni Colonna nobly enters there alone, where he is killed.

Now I turn to the battle. Around midnight the Colonna moved with a great force from the Monument and gathered in the monastery of San Lorenzo fuori le Mura. The weather was oppressive because of the rain and the intense cold. The barons assembled: Stefano della Colonna, and Janni his son; Pietro de Agabito, who had been Provost of Marseilles and Lord of Genazzano; Messer Jordano de Marini, Cola de Buccio de Vraccia, Sciarretta della Colonna, and many others. They took counsel as to what they ought to do, because Stefano was suffering from a stomach ailment and was trembling like a leaf. Pietro de Agabito had slept a little and dreamt that he saw his lady a widow; she wept and tore herself. He was afraid of this dream and wanted to leave the army; he did not want to take part in the battle. Furthermore they had heard the alarm bell sound; they knew that the people were very wrathful and enraged. They were also disturbed by what had happened to Stefano della Colonna, the captain of the whole army, when he went ahead to reconnoiter; he set out alone, mounted on a palfrey and accompanied by a single escort, towards the gate of Rome, and began to call the guard by name in a loud voice. He asked that the gate be opened, giving these reasons: "I am a Roman citizen; I want to return to my house; I come for the Good Estate." He was carrying the banner of the Church and the people. At these words the guard of the gate (his name was Pavolo Buffa, a good archer) answered, "That guard you're calling isn't here. The guards have been changed. My men and I just got here. There's no way you can get in here; the gate is barred. Don't you know how furious the people are at you for disturbing the Good Estate? Don't you hear the bell? I beg you in God's name, get out of here. You don't want to be in such trouble. Just to show that you can't come in, look: I'm throwing out the key."[43] Which fell in a puddle of water that had collected outside because of the bad weather.

43 The door could be unlocked only from the inside.

When the barons had gone over all these things in council, they realized that they could not enter; they decided to depart honorably. Three companies were formed; they were ordered to advance to the gate in front of Rome with trumpets and other instruments sounding, and to turn to the right, and to go back home with great honor. Thus it was done. Already two companies had come, the first and the second, both of infantry and cavalry. Petruccio Freiapane was the leader. When they reached the gate, they sounded their trumpets, made their turn to the right, and returned without incident.

Now the third company came. In it was the multitude of the chivalry: the nobles were there, the valiant were there, and the good horsemen, and all the strength of the army. They had been ordered not to attack under penalty of losing a foot. The vanguard consisted of eight noble barons, among whom was the unfortunate Janni Colonna. This noble vanguard was going a good distance ahead of the rest of the multitude. It was then the dawn of day. The Romans within the gate, not having the key, opened the gate by force in order to go out to battle. Great was the noise from the blows of the hatchets, great was the confusion and the shouting. The right gate was opened, the left remained barred. Janni Colonna, as he approached the gate, misinterpreted the noise within and the disorderly way the gates were being opened; he decided that his friends had been making the noise and had broken down the door by force. And so he quickly took up his shield and, with a lance at his side, spurred his horse, running hard, like a true baron; he did not hold back; he burst through the city gate. Lord, how he terrified the people! All the knights of Rome turned to flee before him; likewise all the people turned and fled, for the space of almost half a crossbow shot. In spite of this Janni Colonna was not followed by his friends; he remained there alone as if he had been called to Judgment. Then the Romans, realizing that he was alone, regained their vigor. Furthermore there was his own bad luck. His war horse carried him into a pit near the left-hand side of the gate. In this pit he was thrown by his horse, and realizing his misfortune he asked pity of the people, and begged them in God's name not to strip him of his armor. What more is there for me to say? There he was stripped, and wounded three times he died. Fonneruglia de Treio was the first to strike him. Janni Colonna was a young man of great diligence; his beard had not yet begun to grow; his fame and glory resounded throughout the world. He lay naked, supine, stabbed, dead, on top of a little mound near the city wall, inside the gate. His hair was covered with mud; he could scarcely be recognized. Now see a wonder. Immediately the pestilential weather changed and the sky began to clear. The sun gave off shining rays; the foggy weather became serene and happy.

CHAPTER THIRTY-FOUR

Stefano della Colonna and many other barons are killed, and the barons' army is routed.

Meanwhile Stefano della Colonna, among the great multitude which was marching past the gate, asked tenderly of his son Janni. He was answered, "We don't know what he's done or where he's gone." Then Stefano suspected that he had entered the gate. Therefore he spurred his horse and entered the gate alone, and saw his son lying on the ground, in the midst of a crowd of people who were killing him, between the pit and the swamp of water. Then Stefano, fearing for his own life, turned around and came out of the gate. His rational mind abandoned him, he was dazed; his love for his son conquered him. He did not speak a word; again he turned and entered the gate to see if he could possibly rescue his son. But as soon as he got near enough he realized that his son was dead; then he thought of his own safety. He turned back in sorrow; as he was going out of the gate a huge stone came down from the turret above and struck him on the shoulders and on the back of his horse. Now lances followed, thrown from this side and that. The horse was struck in the chest by a lance and kicked and bucked so often that Stefano could not keep to the saddle; he fell to the ground. The people poured out, and he was killed in front of the gate, in the middle of the street, in the place where the images are on the wall. There he lay naked to the gaze of all the people and passers-by. He had lost one of his feet; he was covered with wounds. Between his nose and eyes he had a wound so terrible that it looked like the cleft of a wolf's jaws. His son Janni had only two wounds, one in the groin and one in the chest.

Now the people came out in a rage, without order or discipline. They were looking for someone to kill. The young men encountered Pietro de Agabito della Colonna, the Provost of Marseilles, who was coming up behind. He was a cleric; this was the only time he had ever borne arms. He had fallen from his horse; he could not move freely because of the slippery ground; he fled into a nearby vineyard. He was bald and aged; he prayed in God's name that they pardon him. His prayers were useless; first they took his money, then they disarmed him, and then they took his life. He lay in the vineyard, naked, dead, bald, fat: he did not look like a man of war. Near him in the vineyard lay another baron, Pannolfo of the Lords of Belvedere. In a short space of time about twelve were dead. They lay supine. All the rest of the multitude, both infantry and cavalry, left their weapons here and there in their fear and disorder. They did not look back; not one of them struck a blow. Messer Jordano whipped up his horse and did not stop till he reached Marino. The whole multitude was beaten; the enemy were driven out. And those who had been illustrious senators lay dead on the ground, before the eyes of all the passers-by and all the people, until the ninth hour.

Indeed at one point the standard of the Tribune fell to the ground. The Tribune stood in terror with his eyes raised to heaven. The only words he said were these : "Ah, God, have you betrayed me?"

CHAPTER THIRTY-FIVE

The Tribune returns in triumph and lays down his crown and scepter in the Aracoeli. He allows no honor to be paid to the corpses of the three Colonna.

After the people had won their victory, the Tribune had the silver trumpets sounded and with great glory and triumph assembled his army. He placed on his head his crown of silver and of olive branches, and returned triumphant with all the people to Santa Maria d'Aracoeli and there offered his steel scepter and crown of olive to the Virgin Mary. He placed the scepter and crown before that venerable image in the house of the Minorites. After that he never carried the scepter, nor the crown, nor the banner over his head. Then he spoke to the assembled people and said that he wanted to return his sword to its sheath, and drew his sword and wiped it on his clothing and said, "I have cut off an ear from the head that neither the Pope nor the Emperor could touch."

The three bodies, covered with golden mantles, were carried into Santa Maria by the friars, into the chapel of the Colonna. The countesses came with a multitude of women, hair torn, to keen and mourn over the dead, over the bodies of Stefano, Janni, and Pietro de Agabito. The Tribune had them driven away, and refused to allow any honor or obsequies, saying, "If they provoke me any further I shall have these three cursed corpses thrown into the pit of the hanged men, since they are perjurers and do not deserve to be buried." Then the three bodies were secretly carried to the church of San Silvestro in Capite, and there they were buried by the nuns without lament.

Among the other dead citizens were Cola Pali de Molara, Messer Jordano delli Aretini, Cola Farfaro, Polo de Libano, and many other gentlemen of Rome, Orvieto, and other towns near Rome, friends of the dead men mentioned above. The prisoners were put in the Campidoglio.

CHAPTER THIRTY-SIX

The Tribune is rebuked because he, like Hannibal, did not know how to use this victory.

At this point I want to digress a little from my material. The eloquent historian Livy writes that there once arose in Africa a captain, the best the world has ever seen, named Hannibal of Carthage.[44] This Hannibal broke the peace with the Romans, and destroyed the city of Sagunza in Spain, to the spite and shame of the Senate of Rome. Then he crossed the Alps, and entered Piedmont and then Lombardy, and there defeated the Roman consul Sempronius at a river called Ticino, near Pavia. Then he entered Tuscany, and there at the Lake of Perugia he defeated the army of Rome and beheaded the consul Flaminius. Then he planned to attack Spoleto, but could not capture it; he

44 Recounted, apparently from memory, from Books 21 and 22 of Livy. There are several errors in the Chronicler's version, the most glaring of which is the alleged three-year interval between the Battle of Lake Trasimene (the "Lake of Perugia") and the Battle of Cannae.

turned into Campagna, to Monte Cassino, and there Fabius the wise met him at the frontier with a great army, and held him at bay for three years.

After three years the captains were changed: Fabius was dismissed; there were two captains, Aemilius Paulus for the nobles and Terentius Varro for the plebeians. So clever and energetic was Hannibal that he lifted these two captains by their feet and led them with all their forces of cavalry and infantry as far as Puglia, to a river called Volturno, and there defeated the people of Rome. He defeated two armies. One of the commanders, Aemilius Paulus, died there; eighty senators died; Servilius, who had been consul the year before, died; tribunes and nobles died; forty-four thousand infantrymen died; eight thousand eight hundred cavalrymen died; ten thousand prisoners were taken. An infinite amount of booty was taken: horses and arms, gold and silver. The reins and the covers of the Romans' horses were all worked with gold. Rome was terribly bereaved.

After this battle the hour was late; the sun was going down. The victorious Hannibal was very happy. The leaders of the army gathered around him and joyfully celebrated the triumph they had won that day. Then they asked him to allow them and their cavalry to rest that night and the following day, since they were tired and worn out. Among the leaders was a valiant man named Maharbal, who was Duke and leader of the cavalry. He appeared before Hannibal and said, "Hannibal, I do not believe that you should allow yourself or your cavalrymen to rest. Do you want to know what you have won in this battle today? Five days from now you will feast and make merry in the Campidoglio as a conqueror if you follow up your fortune without delay. So give yourself no rest: move your cavalry and your troops; give them no rest. Let us go to Rome; we will find Rome defenseless, with the gates open; you will be lord and master. Better that the Romans say Hannibal has come than Hannibal is coming."

To these words Hannibal answered, "I commend your good will, Maharbal, but the night has counsel. I want to think a little and take counsel." Maharbal replied, "Hannibal, Hannibal, you know with your genius how to win, but you don't know how to use victory." So Livy says that this delay brought salvation to the people of Rome; it freed the Romans from slavery and snatched back the Empire from the hands of the Africans to whom it had fallen.

Now to the proposal: if Cola de Rienzi, Tribune, had followed up his victory, if he had ridden to Marino, he would have captured the castle of Marino and utterly destroyed Messer Jordano, who would never again have lifted up his head, and the people of Rome would have remained free and untroubled.

CHAPTER THIRTY-SEVEN

The Tribune makes his son Lorenzo Knight of the Victory; he begins to be proud and tyrannical, and frees the Prefect. Jordano da Marini harries Rome and many disorders arise.

I will now tell you how the Tribune fell from power. The morning after the battle all the Roman knights, whom he called the Holy Militia, were summoned, and he said to them, "I want to give you double pay; come with me." No one knew that he planned to do. Sounding the trumpets, he went to the battleground, bringing with him his son Lorienzo. In the place where Stefano had died a puddle of water still remained. When they arrived, he had his son dismount, and he sprinkled over him some water from that puddle, which was mixed with Stefano's blood, saying, "You will be Knight of the Victory." All the others were amazed; he also ordered the stunned Constables of the cavalry to dub his son with the flat of their swords. Then he returned to the Campidoglio and said, "Go on your way. What we have done is for the common good. We all have to be Romans; it behooves both you and us to fight for our country." The knights were deeply shocked; after this they refused to carry arms for him again.

Then people began to hate the Tribune; they spoke ill of him and said that he was very arrogant. He began to behave wickedly and to abandon his honest dress; he dressed in clothing like that of an Asian tyrant. Now it became clear that he wanted to rule by force and tyranny; he began taking money from the abbeys' revenues; he arrested people who had money and took from those who had money; he imposed silence upon them. He did not hold public meetings so often because he feared the wrath of the people. He became ruddy and fleshy; he ate better and slept better. Then he released the Prefect, because his health was bad; he kept his son as a hostage.

Then the people began to desert him, and fewer barons came to court for communal business than before. He imposed a salt tax; he wanted money for soldiers. But Messer Jordano de Marini kept raiding every day, and ravaged and robbed. People murmured about the robberies. It was autumn, after the vintage; grain was expensive: the price of a *rubbio*[45] of grain was seven pounds. The Tribune took money from those who had it; Messer Jordano robbed; the people were very dissatisfied. The Cardinal Legate, who was mentioned above, cursed the Tribune and proclaimed him a heretic, and then plotted with the lords, Luca Saviello and Sciarretta della Colonna, and gave them all his support. Then the roads were blockaded; the administrators of the neighboring towns brought no grain to Rome; every day a tumult arose.

45 A unit of dry measure which equals approximately 300 liters.

CHAPTER THIRTY-EIGHT

The Count Messer Janni Pipino, who was living in Rome at that time, stirs up the people, and Cola and his wife flee Rome. He wanders from one place to another, and in Rome is painted as a traitor and condemned as a heretic by the Pope's Legate.

At that time in Rome there was a Count, an exile from the Kingdom,[46] named Messer Janni Pipino, Paladin of Altamura, Count of Minervino. This Paladin was staying in Rome because the Princes of Naples could not endure his excesses and arrogance. He was living in Rome with his family. At this time Messer the Count Paladin had a barricade thrown up in the Colonna region. He was the ringleader of the overthrow of the government in Rome. The barricade was thrown up under the arch of San Salvatore in Pesoli. All night and all day the bell of Sant'Angelo in Pescheria sounded the alarm. It was rung by a Jew. No one gathered to break down the barricade.

The Tribune immediately sent a detachment of cavalry to the barricade. A Constable named Scarpetta, while he was fighting there, was killed by a lance. When the Tribune learned that Scarpetta was dead, and that the people were not gathering at his alarm, although the bell of Sant'Angelo in Pescheria was ringing, he sighed deeply; he trembled; he wept; he did not know what to do. He lost all heart; he was as timid as a little boy; he could scarcely speak; he thought that ambushers were posted against him in the midst of the city. This was not true, because no rebel had appeared. There was no one who raised himself against the people; he was just scared stiff. He believed he was close to death. What more should I say? Because he was not

---

46 That is, the Kingdom of Naples.

courageous enough to die in the service of the people, as he had promised he would, the Tribune wept and sighed and addressed the people who happened to be there, saying that he had ruled well and now, because of envy, people were not content with him. "Now in the seventh month I descend from my dominion." When, weeping, he had spoken these words, he mounted his horse, and sounding the silver trumpets, with the imperial insignia, accompanied by armed men, he descended triumphally, and withdrew to the Castel Sant'Angelo. There he remained hidden. His wife left the Lalli Palace in the dress of a Minorite.

When the Tribune descended from his grandeur those who were with him wept, and the miserable people wept. His chamber was found to be full of great ornaments, letters, and messages. You would not have believed it: the barons learned of his fall, but they were still so fearful that it was three days before they were willing to return to Rome; they held back out of fear. The Senators who succeeded the Tribune ruled weakly and painted a picture of the Tribune as a knight, upside down, on the walls of the Palace of the Campidoglio. They also painted Cecco Mancino, his Notary and Chancellor; they painted his nephew Conte, who surrendered the Castle of Civitavecchia.

The Cardinal Legate entered Rome and started proceedings against the Tribune; he damned the majority of his actions, and said that he was a heretic. Then Cola de Rienzi departed in secret, and went to the Emperor Charles in Bohemia, and stayed in Prague, the royal city. From there he went to the Pope in Avignon, and there succeeded in having the charges against him withdrawn; he was made Senator of Rome by the Pope, and returned to Rome, and did great and memorable deeds, as will be described. Then finally he was killed by the people, and great judgment was passed upon him, as will be related in the Chapter on his return to Italy.

The Paladin who subverted Rome and the Good Estate, by a worthy judgment of God, came to a bad end and died disgracefully. Eight years after these events he was hanged by the gullet in Puglia, in his own town, called Altamura, where he was Paladin. His head was crowned with a paper miter, on which was written: "Messer Janni Pipino, Knight of Altamura, Paladin, Count of Minervino, Lord of Bari, liberator of the people of Rome." Before he was hanged he protested violently, saying, "I am of too high birth to be hanged; I have made no counterfeit money; I should not be wearing a miter. If I must die for my misdeeds, cut off my head." This was the answer of the Princes: "For your disgusting deeds King Robert put you in prison for life. King Andrew freed you and died bitterly as a result. You could not have escaped the vengeance of the Princes. But Rome took you in, and you were saved; and you took away their Good Estate. After you returned to favor with the Princes, you made yourself chief of a great company; you gave asylum in your towns to archers and robbers; you burnt; you robbed; you preyed on all the Kingdom; you made yourself King of Puglia. Therefore it is fitting that your life have a foul and disgraceful end, for this is what you deserve."

These are the first acts of Cola de Rienzi, who wished to be called Tribune August.

BOOK TWO

ON THE SEMICENTENNIAL JUBILEE IN ROME

CHAPTER ONE

Arrival in Rome of the Cardinal of Ceccano, Apostolic Legate, to start the Jubilee.

In the year of our Lord 1350, Pope Clement conceded to the Romans universal indulgence of penalty and guilt for one year. In that year without any impediment all Christendom came to Rome. For this indulgence the Cardinal of Boulogne-sur-Mer was named Legate of Lombardy, and Messer Aniballo de Ceccano was named Cardinal Legate of Rome for the Pope, to rule the people and minister to the pilgrims.

This Cardinal Legate, after enrolling his household staff, left Avignon and proceeded into Lombardy. Messer Janni Visconte, Archbishop of Milan and Tyrant of Lombardy, came out to greet him and pay his respects. Five war horses covered with scarlet and led by hand walked at the head of the Archbishop's company. When the Legate saw this, he was astonished, and said, "Archbishop, what pomp, what vainglory is this?" The Archbishop answered, "Legate, this is not pomp; I only want the Holy Father to know that he has under him a little clerk who can do a thing or two." This Archbishop could only have gotten these war horses from the Constables whom he had dispersed throughout the cities.

When the Legate, Messer Aniballo, came to Rome, he took up residence in the Papal Palace, and began to see to the government of Rome and the pilgrims. This Messer Aniballo had four unpraiseworthy qualities: first, he was a Campanian; second, he had a squint; third, he was very pompous and full of vainglory; as for the fourth, I prefer to remain silent.

The Cardinal, after he arrived in Rome, became embroiled with the Romans in the following way. He had a camel which he kept with the mules in his baggage train. The people came out one day to see this camel, in the cloister below the Palace. The empty-headed people made a big commotion around the Palace: one man stared at the camel, another touched its hair, another its head, another its testicles; they mounted it; now they wanted to make it go. Great was the whistling; great was the noise. A servant of the Legate was there; he thought badly of such license, and rebuked the people. To rebukes he added threats: he ordered everyone to go outside the barrier. The people refused to obey; they took up handfuls of rocks; they broke the barrier; they made straight for the servant. They hurled rocks at the Palace; they cried out, in the usual way, "Ah, ah, ah, to the patarine!"[1]

At this noise more people came, with clubs and staffs. From the piazza of St. Peter's the people of Portica[2] came, fully equipped with steel armor, bucklers, breastplates, shields, and bows. There was a great battle at the Palace. The gate was barred; the noise was terrible; rocks flew; javelins and lances were thrown like hailstones. It looked as if they wanted to sack the fortress.

When the Legate heard this, he was amazed and terrified. He stood on the balcony above; he looked down over everything. He did not know what the reason for all this was. He beat his brow and said, "What does this mean? What have I done? Why am I being insulted this way? So this is how you Romans persuade the Holy Father to return to Rome! The Pope would not be lord in this town, not even a proper archpriest. I did not believe that I came here to fight battles. The Romans are the poorest and haughtiest people in the world." He stretched out his hand and

1 I.e., heretic; the name probably comes from a district in Milan where a heretical sect of puritans lived during the twelfth century.
2 Former name of the region around St. Peter's.

signalled that the riot was to cease. Finally Fra Janni de Lucca, Commander of the Holy Ghost, ran up and quieted the irrational citizens. The Cardinal was very frightened. He would rather have stayed in Avignon.

CHAPTER TWO

Actions and authority of the Legate, and how, having been wounded by a javelin, he excommunicates the Tribune, whom he judges to be the author of treason.

This Legate did notable things. He mounted those two beautiful draperies in St. Peter's which are on the side of the choir, offering one to St. John and the other to St. Mary Major. He planned to audit the treasury of St. Peter's. He gave absolution and penance to provinces, cities, and princes. He punished penitentiaries; he deposed and imprisoned them. He created knights; he bestowed dignities and offices. He increased and decreased the term of the pilgrimage; he reduced the fifteen-day pilgrimage to a single day because there were so many people in Rome that they could not have been controlled otherwise.[3] He said pontifical Mass with all ceremony, just as the Pope does. He came to church and returned to the Palace to the sound of silver trumpets.

The Legate wanted to make the fifteen-day pilgrimage and save his soul like the others, but see what happened to him. After Mass one day the Legate mounted his horse to make the pilgrimage. He left St. Peter's and went to St. Paul's; while he was passing through the street which goes from the Portico of the Armenians to Santo Spirito, midway between San Lorenzo in

3 To gain the indulgence a penitent ordinarily had to visit St. Peter's, St. Paul's, and St. John Lateran once a day for fifteen consecutive days.

Piscibus and Sant' Angelo delle Scale,[4] suddenly two javelins came flying through the window-grating of a little house beside San Lorenzo; they were thrown to kill the Legate. One missed him and flew harmlessly through the air; the other struck him on his hat and there stuck fast.

The Cardinal was stunned with such fare. The procession of his servants stopped; they helped him; they fanned him. A huge clamor went up: "Catch him! Catch him!" They ran here and there looking for the assassin. They ran into the house from which the javelins had come. It had a back door; through that door the throwers, having dropped their javelins, had escaped; they mingled with the great crowd that was there for the absolution and were not recognized. No one was found in the house; two javelins were found. The house was torn down. In the ensuing investigation a priest was taken and put to the torture; he never said who the spear-throwers were.

Then the Legate returned home. A pompous man who longed for glory, he realized that he was despised; he burst with pain; he was furious; he could not rest; he beat his hands and said, "Where have I come? To a desert Rome! Better that I should be a little parish priest in Avignon than a great prelate in Rome. They have fought with me at my house in the Palace; they have thrown spears at me. I hardly know what vengance to take." He could not control his wrath. He began a great search for the malefactors; he could never find out who they were.

The Legate was certain that Cola de Rienzi, the Tribune, was responsible. He put the blame on no one else. Then, to gain the Pope's sympathy, he wrote letters to the Holy Father, in which he described his misfortune, telling how he had been attacked and how he had been shot at and almost killed; along with the

4 Though the hospital and church of Santo Spirito are still standing, the other buildings mentioned here no longer exist; they were all in the neighborhood of the modern Via della Conciliazione.

letter he sent the spear. Then, to retaliate, he passed a terrible sentence, cursing the man who had sinned against him. He cursed and excommunicated Cola de Rienzi, along with his fellow-conspirators, calling him a patarine and a madman; he annulled all his deeds, and called down on him the worst curses he could think of; he deprived the culprits of offices and benefits and dignities, denying them fire and water; he left nothing un-done to confound his enemies. As a man of law he knew how great the crime was and how much punishment it deserved. From this time on the Legate always wore a steel helmet under his hat and a strong breastplate under his cloak.

While these things were going on the Cardinal of San Crisogono happened to be in Rome; he was a Frenchman, a great prelate and a great baron. He appeared before Messer Aniballo to console him, and said, "Anyone who wishes to reform Rome will have to tear everything down and then build it up again from scratch." After saying this he whipped up his horse and returned to his legation.

CHAPTER THREE

Death of the Cardinal Legate and description of the fate of his nephews.

Now I will tell you how the Legate died. It was in the month of July; the heat was terrible. At the Pope's command Messer Aniballo left Rome and went to Naples, to investigate the desolation of the Kingdom of Puglia, which was in desperation, as will be described later.[5] The Legate willingly left Rome for Campagna; he visited Ceccano, his homeland, and passed from

5 Apparently a reference to Ch. 19 (now lost) of the complete chronicle.

there to Monte Cassino and arrived at San Germano, where he stopped.

The next day he left San Germano. After a short journey he came to a nearby castle, where he stayed. As is usual gifts were sent to him from all sides, including many flasks of excellent wine. There are those who say that this wine was poisoned, since all the casks there had been poisoned in the hope of destroying the Great Company that was roaming the countryside.[6] This is not likely. Only a madman would want to poison his own wine.

Of these diverse wines the Cardinal, who was hot from his ride, drank, and drank well, because he was thirsty. He was one of the good drinkers who will inherit the Church of God. This man of Campagna sat at table in the dining hall. He summoned his whole household. He was happy and lighthearted as he dined. It was his habit after meals to drink fresh ewe's milk, in order to refresh himself, according to the advice of his two physicians who were there, Master Guido da Prato and Master Mattheo da Viterbo. He wished to keep to this custom. One of the servants went out to the flocks in the field and there milked the ewes. He returned to the dinner after he had filled a large silver basin with milk. The Cardinal waited a long time, until this milk was prepared and set before him. When it arrived, he sat before it with his spoon and began to eat; he took a stomach full. Corruptible food. Long after the meal the milk was followed by cucumbers, and to refresh himself he ate some of these soaked in vinegar, following the orders of the said physicians. When night came, he went to bed. He found no rest; he could not sleep. The food remained in his stomach, crude and un-digested. In the morning he arose weary, despite his short ride of the day before. The first place he came to was the Villa of San Giorgio. There he stayed, since he could go no further on horse-

6 Following Muratori's reading. The Great Company appears to have been that of Janni Pipino, Paladin of Altamura, who was described in 1.38 (above).

back. He ate nothing that evening; that night he passed from this life.

There was great sorrow in his company. They were like lost lambs abandoned by the shepherd, for two reasons: first, all their baggage had been taken from them by the barons of the neighborhood, and second, one of the Cardinal's two nephews had died. His whole household was suddenly taken sick: that one died, this one died; the whole household died; not a man escaped. Some died in Campagna; some in Rome; some in Viterbo. Messer Janni, the other nephew, died in Santo Spirito in Rome. There wasn't a dog left pissing on the wall.[7]

Hear the news: the Papal Legate died in the Villa of San Giorgio while on a journey; after him his nephew died, and his whole household, in the year of our Lord 1350, during the Jubilee. The Legate's body was opened; it was fat inside, as if he had been an unweaned calf. The hollow of the belly was filled with clear wax. The body was anointed with aloe and dressed in the habit of a Minorite and put in a box on top of a mule like a load of baggage. He returned to Rome by the road on which he had come. He came to St. Peter's without company, without mourning, without clergy; the tomb in his chapel was opened without ceremony; there he was thrown in, not laid in. And he was thrown in so that he fell on his face and so on his face he remained.

Then consider: what is human life? What is the world's glory? What is honor? A pompous man, a high prelate, who longed for money, honors, great apartments, and honorable company, lies alone in the garment of poverty, shut up in his tomb, and despite all his riches a common servant did not even take the trouble to straighten out his corpse on its back the way it ought to be.

7 This sentence, written in Latin, echoes 1 *Kings* 25:22: "May God do so and so, and add more to the foes of David, if I leave of all that belong to him till the morning, any that pisseth against the wall" (Douay).

BOOK THREE

HOW THE SENATOR WAS STONED TO DEATH BY THE ROMANS, AND OF THE
MAGNIFICENT DEEDS DONE BY MESSER EGIDIO CONCHESE OF SPAIN,
CARDINAL LEGATE, TO RECOVER THE PATRIMONY,
THE MARCH OF ANCONA, AND ROMAGNA.

CHAPTER ONE

The Senator of Rome is stoned to death by the people for having starved the city.

When Pope Benedict died, Innocent, formerly Cardinal of Clermont, a secular priest of the habit of St. Peter, was elected Pope.[1] After Pope Innocent's election God wreaked a terrible vengeance on those who had seized the Senate of Rome from him.[2] It was the year of our Lord thirteen hundred fifty-three. During Lent, on a Saturday in February, a call suddenly arose in the market in Rome: "The people! The people!" At this call the Romans gathered. They ran here and there as if a demon had kindled their furor; they threw rocks at the Palace; they plundered whatever they found, especially the Senator's horses.

When the Senator, Vertuollo delli Orzini, heard the noise, he decided to escape to his house and save himself. He armed himself completely, with a shining helmet on his head and spurs on his feet like a baron. He went down the Palace steps to mount his horse. The cries and the furor were turned on the unfortunate Senator. Then stones and rocks rained down on him from above as leaves fall from the trees in autumn. Some people struck him; others threatened to. The Senator was stunned by the blows; his armor was not strong enough to protect him. But he managed to go on foot as far as the part of the Palace where the image of St. Mary stands. There the storm of rocks finally weakened him. Ruthlessly and lawlessly the people ended his days then and

---

1 "Pope Benedict" is a slip for Pope Clement (VI); "Innocent" is Pope Innocent VI.

2 The current Senators, as had been stated in Ch. 25 (now lost) of the complete chronicle, were ruling without papal ratification.

there, stoning him like a dog, throwing rocks on his head as on St. Stephen. There the Count passed from this life excommunicated. He did not say a single word. He was left there dead and everyone went home. His fellow Senator ingloriously saved himself by sliding down a rope and passing through the postern gate of the Palace with his face veiled and a worn-out cap on his head.

The reason for this great severity was that these two Senators lived like tyrants. They were already infamous for sending grain out of Rome by sea in time of need. Grain was very expensive; the poor people could not endure the hunger and famine. Hungry people do not know how to fear; they do not wait for someone to say, "Do this." This is a fact about famine which has overthrown many powerful people. Another reason could be that God does not permit the goods of the Church to be violated. Valerius Maximus speaks of this.[3] He gives the example of Dionysius, Tyrant of Sicily, who cut off the golden hair and beards of his gods, saying that the gods should not look like bearded goats. For this insult to his gods he lived in fear and trembling for the rest of his life, and after his death his son was reduced to such misery that he earned his living by teaching the alphabet to boys. Perhaps that was all he knew.[4] Now see a wonder: after it became known that the Senator had been stoned to death, the famine suddenly ceased throughout the country, and the price of grain became reasonable.

3 Valerius Maximus, 1.1. Ext.3.
4 The Chronicler's gibe is prompted by his own misunderstanding of Valerius Maximus' Latin phrase *litteras ... docuit* (6.9. Ext.6). This of course means "taught literature"; the Chronicler understands it to mean "taught the alphabet".

CHAPTER TWO

Cardinal Egidio Conchese of Spain, sent into Italy by Pope Innocent as his Legate, forces Janni di Vico to restore Viterbo, Marta, and Canino, which he had usurped, to the Church.

The first thing Pope Innocent wished to do was to force the tyrants to restore the stolen property, the goods of the Church, which they had usurped. To accomplish this he sent Cardinal Egidio Conchese of Spain into Italy as his Legate. The feats of this Don Egidio show what a good warrior he was. First he was a knight with golden spurs, then Archdeacon of Conche; he was so energetic that he became Gonfalonier of the King of Castile. He was present in person at the fall of Tarifa in Spain, as was said above.[5]

The Legate, Don Egidio, came down to the Patrimony: to Montefiascone, Acquapendente, and Bolsena. All the other towns were occupied by Janni de Vico, Prefect of Viterbo; he held Terni, Amelia, Narni, Orvieto, Viterbo, Marta, and Canino. He had made a great name for himself; he was trying to subvert Perugia. The Legate was astonished when he found so few towns subject to the Church. Nevertheless he decided to speak with the Prefect. He sent for him and they met. The Prefect had a bad habit of agreeing immediately to whatever was asked of him, saying, "It will be done; it pleases us well," and afterwards refusing to keep his word. The more he promised you the less attention he paid to you. Through long habit he behaved this way with the Legate; he did not know how to do otherwise. At their meeting the Legate said, "Prefect, what do you want?" The Prefect answered, "Whatever pleases you." The Legate said, "I

5 The capture of the city of Tarifa from the Muslims was described in Ch. 11 of the complete chronicle. Egidio Conchese is more commonly known as Gil d'Albornoz.

want you to restore to the Church what is hers and keep what is yours." The Prefect said, "I will do it freely. I am content." And he placed his seal on a paper on which articles to this effect were written. He turned around and went back to Viterbo.

The Prefect did not keep one of his promises; he said, "I will not keep any of them." He added, "The Legate has fifty priests and chaplains in his company; my servant boys are enough to stand against his priests." Inevitably this reached the ears of the Legate, who answered, "It will soon be clear that my priests are braver than the Prefect and his boys."

When the Legate learned of the Prefect's hardened soul and his perverse obstinate mind, he did not declare a crusade against him, since he did not seem worth it, but enlisted the aid of the League of Tuscany: of Perugia, Florence, and Siena. He enrolled a great army which he led personally. Cola de Rienzi, who, as was said before, had been absolved at Avignon by the Pope, was in this army. The Prefect ignored the host of soldiers. Then the people of Rome came out to join them; Janni, Count of Valmontone, was the captain. He began to devastate a third of Viterbo; he destroyed vineyards, olive orchards, and trees; he levelled everything. The people of Viterbo blamed the Prefect; Ranieri de Busa was harassing him as well. The Prefect, a tyrant who doubted his own citizens, feared that worse was in store for him. He took wiser counsel and placed himself in the embrace and lap of the Church, and returned what he had taken. He surrendered Viterbo, Orvieto, Marta, and Canino. He was allowed to keep his own castles, and Corneto, Civitavecchia, and Rispampani as well.

A short time afterwards Jordano delli Orzini took Corneto from him in broad daylight. The Prefect complained to the Legate, saying that he had been cheated because he had been driven out of Viterbo. The Legate answered, "Prefect, you suffer no wrong." He showed him the sealed agreement, which read,

"I will restore what is not mine and keep what is my own." On hearing this the Prefect was quiet.

In Viterbo the Legate built a beautiful castle, furnished with many towers, palaces, and apartments, to strengthen and protect the Church of Rome. This castle stands and grows to our own day. It lies near the Montefiascone gate; it has a good supply of water, and moats filled with water surround it.

CHAPTER THREE

The Legate, having recovered Narni and Amelia, moves against the Malatesti in the March, where Galeotto Malatesta surrenders to him.

Once he had finished organizing the Patrimony, the Legate stayed in Orvieto for a while; he reconciled Orvieto and its district, which were very corrupt. Then he took Narni, then Amelia, and from there went on to do greater deeds: to restore order in the March, and to lower the pride of the Malatesta. Messer Malatesta was a powerful tyrant and one of the most skilful warriors of Romagna. He was lord over many cities and castles; he ruled most of the March of Ancona, whether through love or force. His brother, Messer Galiotto, guarded the frontiers and ruled the noble city of Ancona.

When Messer Galiotto heard that the Legate was approaching the lands of the March, he gathered a great multitude, more than three thousand knights; he marched from Ancona to Recanati to meet the Legate, along with Gentile da Magliano of Fermo and many other Corporals of the March. There he waited, and announced to the Legate that he might just as well not have come: he could neither equal the Malatesti nor defeat them. In reply the Legate sent a note which contained only the following words: "From good warriors good peacemakers, from good peacemakers good warriors." Messer Galiotto answered, "Tell the Legate not to endanger so many people; I will meet him on the field in single combat." The Legate answered, "Go, tell him: here I am, ready on the field; there I will meet him myself, face to face. Let him stay where he is." Messer Galiotto answered, "Go tell my lord the Legate that I will not meet him face to face; even if I should win, it would be the end of me, for he is an aged man, a prelate, fit only for the paternal care of souls."

At that time a young gentleman of the March, named Nicola da Buscareto, was with the Legate; he was present at these embassies, and said, "Lord Legate, you don't realize that the Malatesti are finished. You don't see that in his own words Messer Galiotto is broken and defeated; he cannot oppose you; we have won. Legate, don't let up; keep harrying the Malatesti of Rimini, now that Galiotto is already beaten. He's lost his nerve. His own words show me this." These words fired the Legate to press the Malatesti even harder.

The Legate had many good soldiers with him, many Corporals of the March: Messer Lomo da Esci, Jumentaro dalla Pira, the Lord of Cagli, Messer Redolfo de Camerino, and Esmeduccio de Santo Severino. He also had the noble German soldiers whom the Emperor had given to him. The Emperor Charles, of whom more will be said later,[6] was in Rome in those days. He had been crowned; all Tuscany, Lombardy, Romagna, and Germany had paid homage to him. The Legate asked this Emperor for help, and the Emperor sent him the cavalrymen whom the communes of Perugia and Florence had assigned to him. Messer Charles also sent him many tested barons of Germany.

6 In Ch. 28 (now lost) of the complete chronicle.

Meanwhile the Legate assembled his army on the field. Messer Galiotto Malatesta had retreated into a strong town called Paterno, between Macerata and Ancona, when behold: suddenly the noble imperial army came up behind him: Germans and Tuscans, Counts of Germany experienced in war, many crested helmets, bagpipes and kettledrums sounding. They had never rested once they began their march. When Messer Galiotto heard that these allies had joined the Legate, he lost his resolution and his strength. He was helpless; he admitted defeat; he surrendered, begging the Legate for mercy. The Legate held him captive along with his whole army.

CHAPTER FOUR

Malatesta, in order to recover his brother, peacefully restores to the Legate the Church property he had seized. The cruel and tyrannical actions of Francesco Ordelaffi of Forlì are recounted.

Messer Malatesta, in order to recover his brother, submitted to the Legate, freely surrendering to him the city of Ancona and all the towns which he held in the March and in Romagna. Thus the Church acquired the noble city of Ancona, a seaport rich in trade and revenues. There the Legate built two beautiful fortresses which stand to this day. Then he made one of his nephews Marquis and sent him to Macerata as governor of the March. He provided for the Malatesti indulgently and wisely, to enable them to live honorably and nobly from their rents. He granted them four good and famous cities, Rimini, Fano, Pesaro, and Fossombrone, four notable and powerful towns. Then he made them Captains of the Church against rebels.

After this the Legate went on to greater deeds and undertakings. There was a perfidious patarine dog in Romagna, a rebel against the holy Church. He had been excommunicated for thirty years, his country interdicted, no Mass sung. He held many towns which belonged to the Church: the cities of Forli, Cesena, Forlimpopolo, Castrocaro, Bertinoro, Imola, and Giaggiolo. He was tyrant over all these, along with many other castles and communes which belonged to the local inhabitants. This Francesco delli Ordelaffi was a desperate man; he had an insane hatred against prelates, never forgetting that earlier he had been mistreated by the former Legate, Messer Bettrannio dallo Poijetto, Cardinal of Ostia, as was said above.[7] He refused to submit to priests any longer. He was a perfidious obstinate tyrant.

This Francesco, when he heard the bell ring for his excommunication, immediately had the other bells rung and excommunicated the Pope and the Cardinals, and, what was worse, he had stuffed paper effigies of the Pope and the Cardinals burnt in the piazza. Conversing with his well-born friends he said, "So: we are excommunicated; our bread, though, and our meat, and the wine we drink won't taste any the worse or be any the less wholesome for that." He treated the priests and the monks in the following way. The bishop who pronounced the excommunication was insulted and driven from the city. Then the Captain forced the clergy to say Mass. Most of them did, despite the interdict. Fourteen clerics, seven religious and seven secular, refused to say Mass and received holy martyrdom: seven of them were hanged by the gullet and seven of them were flayed. But Francesco was closely bound to the people of Forli, and dearly loved; he behaved as if he were pious and charitable: he gave dowries to orphans, found husbands for girls, and helped those of the poor people who were his friends.

---

7 In Ch. 5 of the complete chronicle.

CHAPTER FIVE

The Legate, after having taken up arms against Ordelaffi, is recalled by the Pope, who sends the Abbot of Burgundy as new Legate.

Now I turn to the war. Don Gilio Conchese of Spain established his headquarters and residence in Ancona, and to strengthen his forces proclaimed a crusade. I myself heard it announced: remission of penalty and guilt to whoever took the cross or gave aid. Now the Legate moved against the dog Captain of Forlì, Francesco delli Ordelaffi. Before setting up his camp he prepared everything necessary for the army.

The Legate sent bishops, knights, and other worthy people to persuade the Captain not to persevere in his error. He heard the exhortations in silence; that night he made a foray from Forlì and plundered the lands of the Church; he took loot and prisoners. He made no other response. The Legate, recognizing the hardened heart of Ordelaffi, set up camp against the city of Cesena. The Malatesti were Corporals and leaders of the army. There were twelve thousand crusaders and thirty thousand mercenaries; out of these two separate armies were formed. The army made great devastation and damage: at the sound of trumpets three thousand plunderers with banners ravaged the enemy land and then withdrew: a memorable deed. Meanwhile the Holy Father sent express letters ordering Don Gilio to return to Provence. The reason for this was that the Count of Savoy, with his great company of three thousand soldiers, was plundering the whole of Provence: he was seizing towns, robbing, and kidnapping people. Before Don Gilio left another Legate arrived, a wealthy French landowner, strong and powerful.

The Captain had a son named Messer Janni and another named Messer Lodovico. Messer Lodovico approached his father and humbly beseeched him, saying, "Father, in God's name I beg you not to contend with the Church, and not to stand against God. Let us obey these commands; let us be obedient. I am certain that the Legate is considerate; he will treat us as well as he has treated the Malatesti. He will allow us enough to live well and honorably." To these humble words the proud father replied, "You are a bastard, or else you were switched at baptism to spite me." The son, after hearing his father's violent answer, turned to leave. Then his father threw a long naked knife at his back, and wounded him in the kidneys; before midnight his son Lodovico died from this wound.

While the new Legate, the Abbot, prepared himself for war, Messer Gilio was not idle. He attacked Cesena, and set up three bastions at intervals of ten miles each. The Legates returned to Rimini.

CHAPTER SIX

Cesena is taken by the Legate through the work of four citizens.

Madonna Cia, the wife of the Captain of Forlì, was in Cesena, inside the castle, with her nephews and a large group of mercenaries. To this Madonna Cia the Captain wrote a letter which said, "Cia, be cautious and take good care of the city of Cesena." Madonna Cia replied, "My lord, be content to take good care of Forlì, and I shall take good care of Cesena." The Captain wrote another letter, the gist of which was, "Cia, we command you to cut off the heads of four plebeians of Cesena, Janni Zaganella, Jacovo delli Vastardi, Palazzino, and Bertonuccio, all Guelfs, whose loyalty we suspect."

When the lady received this letter, she did not follow her husband's orders at once. She investigated these four citizens with the greatest care and diligence, and found that they were good and loyal men. She took counsel with two of her husband's most loyal friends, Scaraglino, a nobleman, and Giorgio delli Tumberti. She showed them the letter, and they said, "Madam, we find no reason that these men should lose their lives. We know of no plots they are forming. If these men lose their lives, the people are liable to become indignant. We suggest, therefore, that you postpone this judgment. Meanwhile we shall watch their behavior closely. At the least sign of trouble we shall take immediate action: we shall arrest them and execute them after an open trial." The lady followed the advice of her husband's two noble friends, and put aside her investigation into sedition.

All this was done in secret, and in secret it was revealed to the four plebeians. Then they formed a conspiracy and planned a revolution in the city. Janni Zaganella made the arrangements among his friends. He rode on his pony throughout the town, stirring up one man after another. One morning, when the plot was still recent, Jacovo delli Vastardi and his neighbors ran to the gate which is called Troygate and seized it. Bertonuccio and Palazzino aroused the people and barricaded the city; then they sent two hostlers to the Hungarian soldiers who were occupying the bastions at Savignano nearby. They came quickly.

When Madonna Cia heard the commotion, she knew that the people had arisen; she immediately ordered her mercenaries, cavalry and infantry, to take up their arms and overrun the city. But this was impossible: the town was barricaded, the people armed, the city gate taken, the towers fortified, and furthermore the knights had come to the aid of the people. There in the setting of the sun were eight hundred Hungarian archers, who had been occupying the bastions at Savignano; they came flying, a lively people, drawn up in battle order. They did not enter Cesena, but circled the city, now approaching, now withdrawing, to encourage the citizens. Seeing this Madonna Cia withdrew her mercenaries, retreated to the citadel, and there held out. This citadel is part of the city; it is surrounded by a strong wall, and contains the communal piazza, the palace, the tower, and great private houses; it is set rather high above the city, which is low-lying. Madonna Cia, angry at her loss, turned her wrath on the two counsellors, her husband's friends, Giorgio delli Tumberti and Scaraglino; she had them beheaded. Her husband disapproved of this deed.

CHAPTER SEVEN

Capture of the citadel of Cesena and imprisonment of Madonna Cia, wife of Ordelaffi.

When dawn broke on the next day, behold: the Malatesti arrived with a great army to help the citizens. Troygate was surrendered to them, and they entered Cesena. Now Madonna Cia was besieged in the citadel. Then the Fiumone castle was surrendered. The Malatesti fought hard at the citadel: they made forays, they threw fire inside, they raised catapults and threw rocks and stones. It was useless: the defenders had plenty of water, and there was a strong tower above the citadel gate.

The Legate ordered undermining, a hard, expensive, and time-consuming job. A tunnel was dug under the cistern of the citadel, the cistern was broken, and the water was lost. Then they brought the tunnel under the main tower of the piazza. They set fire to the struts, and the tower collapsed with a great crash. Now the tunnel was extended to the tower above the gate, which protected the citadel's entrance. Madonna Cia, angry at this, did not know what to do. She selected those of the citizens within the citadel whom she most mistrusted and put them in the tower above the gate, saying, "If the tower falls, it falls on you." The tower stood on its struts; it trembled.

Meanwhile the Legate, Don Gilio, was passing through the district with a great company of soldiers; he came to Cesena to see how the tunnelling and the siege works were progressing. Then about five hundred women came pouring out of Cesena, tearing their hair, beating their breasts, weeping, and lamenting. They made a great noise. They fell on their knees before the Legate and pled for mercy. The Legate, not knowing the reason for this bitter weeping, asked why they were doing it. The women answered, "Legate, our husbands, brothers, and kinsmen are imprisoned in the tower above the gate. The tunnel is completed; if the tower falls, the men will perish. Therefore we beg in God's name that you delay setting fire to the struts."

The Legate realized that Madonna Cia doubted herself, that her resolution was broken. He held negotiations with her and recovered the people of Cesena who had been put in the tower. Then they set fire to the tower; in a little while it fell, along with part of the citadel wall. So the wall was breached, and they could enter; nevertheless they entered calmly, not furiously.

The Legate took Madonna Cia prisoner, along with her son and two nephews. Madonna Cia refused to be released, fearful of her husband's quick temper. Rather she begged insistently that the Church protect her. The masters of the tunnelling, the catapults, and the other devices cost three thousand florins a day. The soldiers cost twelve thousand florins a day. The Legate entered Cesena and took the town for the Church. This was how the city of Cesena in Romagna was recovered.

CHAPTER EIGHT

The Legate repeatedly declares a crusade against Ordelaffi, and finally strips him of Faenza and Bertinoro.

Now the Legate prepared to attack the city of Forlì. First he collected a strong and copious army. Meanwhile news spread of the imprisonment of Madonna Cia, who had been sent to Ancona under guard. One of her daughters, a noblewoman, married to a great man of the March, appeared before her father in tears, with her arms folded; falling on her knees she said to him, "Father, my lord, please do not allow my mother, so great a lady, to remain a prisoner in the hands of others. I beg you, do the will of the holy Church." The Captain's only response to these words was this: he seized this daughter of his by the hair and with a knife he parted her head from her body.

After the capture of Cesena the Legate sent to the Captain, saying, "Captain, return what is not yours. I am returning your wife, your son, and your nephews to you." To these words the Captain replied, "Tell the Legate that I used to believe he was a wise man; now I consider him a stupid ox. Tell him that if I had captured him, the way he has captured my people, I would have hanged him by the gullet three days ago." His soul hardened against such a perverse patarine heretic, Don Gilio, the old Legate, departed for Provence. When the company of the Count of Savoy heard that Don Gilio was approaching the borders, it melted away like a bit of snow in the hot sun.

The new Legate, the Abbot of Burgundy, remained in Romagna. This Abbot besieged Forlì with an army of private soldiers. For many years he declared the crusade; the cross was preached through all Italy. He lopped the grain and cut down the vineyards, trees, and olive orchards; he struck at every point, at every hour. Because of this fervent war the Captain and his sworn allies, the Manfredi, lost Faenza; he also lost Bertinoro. Then he retreated to the citadel of Forlì.

During the siege of Forlì many crusaders, who had come to gain indulgence by fighting these schismatics, were captured. The captured crusaders would be brought before Francesco, who would say to them, "You carry the cross; the cross is made of cloth; cloth wears out. I want you to carry crosses which will not wear out." Then a red-hot iron of the form of a cross would be prepared; with it he would brand the soles of their feet, and so, after robbing them, he would let them go. Many other crusaders were captured; to these he would say, "You have come to save your souls; if I let you go perhaps you will return to your earlier sins. It would be better for you to die while in a state of contrition. God will receive you into His city." Saying this, he would have them flayed, hanged, beheaded, impaled, and torn to pieces, to die of various martyrdoms.

The war lasted for many years. To maintain it the crusade was proclaimed many times. Just recently, in the year of our Lord 1358, in January, it was proclaimed in the city of Tivoli.[8]

8 The chapter concludes with the following words, written in Latin: "About this time King John of France was captured by the son of the King of England, in a war that was more a mob than a military action, at a town called ***; he was taken to England and imprisoned for about two years, and finally escaped, with great loss to himself and his kingdom." This may be a later marginal addition; at any rate, it has clearly not been fully incorporated into our text.

BOOK FOUR

SECOND PART OF THE LIFE OF MESSER NICOLA DE RIENZI, IN WHICH
IS CONTAINED HIS RETURN TO ROME AND REASSUMPTION OF POWER
AND THE DEEDS DONE BY HIM AFTER HIS RETURN, AND THE DEATH
DEALT TO HIM BY THE PEOPLE OF ROME.

CHAPTER ONE

Cola, after hiding for seven years in various ways, goes to the Emperor, by whom he is most graciously received.

It was the year of our Lord thirteen fifty-three,[1] on the first day of August, when Cola de Rienzi returned to Rome and was solemnly welcomed. Finally he was killed at the voice of the people. This is how it all happened. After Cola de Rienzi fell from his dominion, he decided to leave Rome and go and appear before the Pope. Before his departure he had a picture painted on the wall of Santa Maria Maddalena[2] in the piazza of the Castel Sant'Angelo, which showed an angel in armor, with the arms of Rome, holding a cross in his hand; above the cross was a dove. The angel was trampling the asp and the basilisk, the lion and the dragon, under his feet.[3] After this picture was painted, the fools of Rome threw mud on it to show their contempt. One evening Cola de Rienzi came in secret, unrecognized, to see the picture before his departure. He saw it and realized that the fools had dishonored it. Then he ordered a lamp to be burnt before it for one year.

At night he left Rome, and went wandering for a long time. It was seven years. He travelled in disguise, in fear of the Roman nobles. He lived like a friar, sleeping in the mountains of Maiella with hermits and penitents. Finally he went to Bohemia, to the Emperor Charles, whose arrival in Rome will be described

1 The year of Cola's return was actually 1354.
2 No longer standing.
3 Cf. *Ps.* 90:13: 'Thou shalt walk upon the asp and the basilisk: and thou shalt trample under foot the lion and the dragon" (Douay).

later,[4] and found him in a city called Prague. There, falling on his knees before the Imperial Majesty, he spoke readily. These are the words of the eloquent speech he delivered before Charles, King of Bohemia, grandson of the Emperor Henry, who had recently been elected Emperor by the Pope:

"Most serene prince, to whom the glory of all the world is granted, I am that Cola whom God in His grace allowed to govern Rome and its territory in peace, justice, and liberty. I was obeyed by Tuscany and Campagna and Marittima; I bridled the arrogance of the nobles and purged their injustice. I am a worm, a frail man, a plant like all the others. I bore in my hand the rod of iron, which through my humility I changed to a rod of wood. But God wished to castigate me. The nobles are pursuing me; they seek my life. Because of envy and because of pride they have driven me from my dominion; they refuse to accept their just punishment. I am of your lineage; I am a bastard son of the Emperor Henry the valiant. To you I flee; to your wings I run, under whose shade and shield a man ought to be safe. I believe that I am safe; I believe that you will defend me. You will not let me die at the hands of tyrants; you will not let me drown in the lake of injustice. And this is as it should be: since you are Emperor, your sword ought to cut down the tyrants. I have seen the prophecy of Fra Agnilo de Montecielo in the mountains of Maiella, and he said that the eagle will kill the crows."[5]

After Cola had spoken, Charles stretched forth his hand and received him graciously, saying that he need have no doubts about anything. When Cola came to Prague it was the first day

4 The arrival in Rome and the coronation of the Emperor Charles IV were described in Ch. 28 (now lost) of the complete chronicle.

5 The Chronicler apparently based this speech on two letters addressed by Cola to the Emperor Charles (*Epistolario* 30 and 31). It is an accurate summary of Cola's apology; his incredible claim to be the bastard son of the Emperor Henry VII was actually made.

of August. He stayed there for some time. He disputed with the masters in theology; he declaimed at length; he spoke of wonderful things. His fluent tongue amazed those Germans, Bohemians, and Slavs; he stupefied everyone. He was not imprisoned, but detained honorably under some guards. Ample food and wine were given to him.

CHAPTER TWO

Cola goes to defend himself in Avignon; there he is imprisoned and later absolved from the sentence of the Cardinal of Ceccano.

After some time he asked the Emperor to allow him to go to Avignon and appear before the Pope, to prove that he was neither a heretic nor a patarine. The Emperor was strongly opposed to this, but finally yielded. Cola de Rienzi said, "Most serene prince, I am going voluntarily to appear before the Holy Father. Therefore, since you are not sending me by force, you are innocent of breaking your oath." As he journeyed from one town to the next, the people arose; crowds gathered; they met him with cries and shouts. They held him back, saying that they wanted to save him from the Pope; they did not want him to go. To all he said, "I am going voluntarily; I am not forced," and thanked them, and thus passed from city to city. Solemn honors were paid to him along the way. When the people saw him, they were amazed; they accompanied him, and thus he arrived in Avignon on the first day of August.[6]

6 As described in a letter of Petrarch (*Fam.* 13.6) Cola's journey to Avignon was hardly so triumphant as it is in our account, nor, as we know from Cola's own correspondence, was his treatment in Prague and Avignon so honorable as the Chronicler claims.

He entered Avignon and appeared before the Pope. There he defended himself, and said that he was not a patarine, nor did he deserve the sentence which the Cardinal and Don Bruno[7] had passed against him; he was willing to undergo examination. At these words the Pope was silent. Cola was imprisoned in a great tower; one of his legs was shackled to a chain which was attached to the ceiling of the tower room. There he stayed, dressed in plain clothing. He had plenty of books: his Livy, his histories of Rome, the Bible, and many other books. He never stopped studying. He had ample nourishment from the Pope's table, which was given to him through godly charity. His deeds were examined and he was found to be a faithful Christian. Then the process and the sentence of Don Bruno and the Cardinal of Ceccano were revoked, and he was absolved, and gained the favor of the Pope, and was released.

CHAPTER THREE

Cola returns to Rome with the Apostolic Legate, where he receives many requests from the Roman people.

When Cola left prison it was the first day of August. A Legate, Don Gilio Conchese, Cardinal of Spain, was going to go to Italy; he prepared himself and enrolled his household. With this Legate Cola de Rienzi left Avignon, purged, blessed, and absolved, and with the Legate he passed through Provence, and arrived in Montefiascone, to recover the Patrimony, as was said before. Among the first towns which surrendered to the Church was Toscanella, and its castle was sold. Cola de Rienzi took part

---

7 I.e., the two Legates, Annibaldo di Ceccano and Bertrand de Déaux, Cardinal of Embrun.

in the capture of this town for the Church, and in the siege of Viterbo, and in all those knightly feats of arms. He had good and honorable clothing and a good horse.

Not only in the army, but in Montefiascone as well, he received so many invitations from the Romans that it is amazing to tell. Every Roman paid court to him. He was visited constantly. A great train of plebeians stretched out behind him. Everyone was astonished, even the Legate, who was deeply impressed by the invitations of the citizens of Rome. They all looked at him in wonder; it seemed amazing to them that he had emerged unharmed from the hands of so many powerful men. In the devastation of Viterbo, as was narrated above, Roman soldiers participated. When the army returned, many Romans gathered to see Cola de Rienzi: plebeians, with great tongues and hearts, greater offers, few results. They said, "Return to your Rome; cure it of its great sickness; be its lord. We will give you aid, favor, and strength. Do not hesitate. You were never so missed nor loved as you are now." This froth the plebeians of Rome gave him; they did not give him one penny.

Cola de Rienzi was moved by these words, and by his innate desire for glory as well. He wished to lay some foundation for himself, from which he could acquire soldiers and assistance, in order to enter Rome. He spoke to the Legate about this. The Legate did not give him one penny. He did, however, order him to be given some provision from the Commune of Perugia, on which he could live justly and honorably. This provision was not enough for Cola to hire soldiers. Therefore he rode to Perugia, where he appeared before the council many times. He spoke well, he declaimed well, he promised better. The councillors listened intently, eager to hear his sweet words. Thus they let themselves be licked like honey. But because the councillors were subject to syndics they had to take good care of the property of their commune. From the Commune of Perugia Cola could not get one cortonese.[8]

CHAPTER FOUR

Cola, thanks to the aid of Messer Arimbaldo and Messer Brettone, is prepared to try his luck again.

In Perugia at that time there were two young Provençals, Messer Arimbaldo, Doctor of Laws, and Messer Brettone, a knight of Narbonne in Provence, blood brothers. These men were blood brothers of the valiant Fra Morreale. Fra Morreale had fought for the King of Hungary; then he became chief of the Great Company; he destroyed many towns in Puglia; he burnt and fired many; he sacked countless communes, and carried off the women. In Tuscany he held Siena, Florence, Arezzo, and many other towns for ransom; he divided the money among his companions. He passed from there to the March and destroyed the Malatesti; he captured Monte Feltrano and Filino, where more than seven hundred peasants died; he burnt and robbed the towns; he held the men for ransom and carried off the women, those who were attractive. He was a Friar of St. John, a zealous and valiant man, whose valor will be described later.

This man had acquired a great deal of money through his robberies and plundering. He had so much money that he could live honorably without further campaigning. He led these two brothers of his to Perugia and had the Commune make provision for them. He deposited his money with the merchants there and ordered his brothers to avoid contention and co-operate with one another; now that he had established them there he intended

8 A coin minted in Cortona (near Perugia).

to devote himself to his Order. Fra Morreale went elsewhere to do his other business.

When Cola de Rienzi heard that Messer Arimbaldo de Narba, a young man and a literate person, was staying in Perugia, he went to his inn and asked to dine with him. When dinner was over, Cola de Rienzi began to speak of the power of the Romans. He wove his tales from Livy and told of Biblical deeds; he opened the fount of his wisdom. Lord, how well he spoke! He would exert all his skill in declamation, and would speak so effectively that everyone would be stupefied by his beautiful speeches; he would lift each man off his feet. Messer Arimbaldo would hold his hand to his cheek and listen in silence. He was astonished by these beautiful speeches; he was amazed at the greatness and valor of the Romans. As the wine warmed, his soul would climb on high. The dreamer pleased the dreamer. Messer Arimbaldo did not know how to live without Cola de Rienzi: he stayed with him, he went with him. They ate the same meal; they slept in the same bed; they planned to do great deeds, to raise up Rome and return it to its pristine glory.

For this they had to get money. Without soldiers it could not be done. They needed at least three thousand florins to start with. Cola persuaded Messer Arimbaldo to pledge three thousand florins, promising that he would repay him, and swearing to make him a Roman citizen and a great honored Captain, whether his brother, Messer Bettrone, liked it or not. So Messer Arimbaldo took four thousand florins from the money which had been deposited with the merchants and gave it to Cola de Rienzi.

Before Messer Arimbaldo handed this money over to Cola de Rienzi, however, he wanted to get permission from his elder brother, Fra Morreale. He sent him a letter, the gist of which was, "Honored Brother, I have gained more in one day than you have in your whole lifetime. I have won the lordship of Rome; it has been promised to me by Messer Cola de Rienzi, Knight, Tribune, who is courted by the Romans and summoned by the people. I am certain that the plan will not fail. I am sure that with the help of your talent this undertaking will come to a happy end. Money is needed to begin this. If you, my brother, agree to it, I shall take four thousand florins from the deposit and go to Rome with a powerful army."

Fra Morreale, when he had read his brother's letter, wrote back. This was the tenor of his reply: "I have considered your proposal for a long time. It is a great and important burden which you are planning to bear. I cannot persuade myself that you will be successful. My mind will not let me; my reason forbids it. Nevertheless do it, and may it go well with you. First of all take care that the four thousand florins are not lost. If you meet with any difficulty, write to me. I shall come with help, with a thousand, with two thousand men, as many as are needed, and I shall do magnificent deeds. Do not hesitate. You and your brother must love and honor one another. Make no noise."

When Messer Arimbaldo received this letter, he was very happy. He and the Tribune prepared themselves for the journey.

CHAPTER FIVE

Cola, made Senator of Rome by the Legate, sets out for the city with the army he has hired.

After Cola de Rienzi received the four thousand florins, he dressed himself richly in elaborate clothing. He followed his own wisdom in outfitting himself: a tunic, a cloak, a cape lined with fur and decorated with fine gold, hemmed with gold, a decorated sword at his side, a decorated horse, golden spurs, and servants newly hired and clothed. Thus outfitted, he returned to Montefiascone to see the Legate. In his company were Messer Bettrone and Messer Arimbaldo de Narba, brothers, with their servants and property.

When Cola appeared before the Legate, he looked completely different; he cut a splendid figure in his scarlet hood and cape of fur-lined scarlet. He swaggered; he shook his head; he moved his head back and forth, as if to say, "Who am I? Am I someone?" Then he raised himself up on his toes; now he went up; now he went down. The Legate was astonished and put some faith in what he said. But he did not give him one penny. Then Cola said, "Legate, make me Senator of Rome. I shall go and prepare the way for you." The Legate made him Senator and sent him on his way.

In order to go to Rome he needed soldiers. Recently Messer Malatesti of Rimini had dismissed his soldiers, sixteen companies, good men. Two hundred fifty soldiers were staying in Perugia looking for work. Wishing to hire these men, Cola de Rienzi sent his messenger. The messenger found the constables and said, "Enlist for two months; you will receive the first month's pay in advance; you will be hired permanently; you will lead Messer Cola de Rienzi, Senator for the Pope, to Rome."

When they heard this the constables went into council. The German constables argued that they ought not to go. They advanced three reasons. The first: "Romans are bad people, proud and arrogant; in this they are unequalled." The second: "This man is a plebeian, poor, of vile condition; he will have nothing to pay us with. So whom shall we serve?" The third: "The Roman aristocrats are opposed to this man's government; if we displease them they will become our enemies. Therefore let us not take this job; this work in Rome will do us no good." This indeed was the answer of the Germans, and it was correct. Germans, when they first come down from Germany, are simple, pure, and guileless. After they have worked among the Italians, they become astute masters, vicious, and skilled in every evil. The Germans were opposed by a Burgundian constable, who said, "Let us take this money and enlist for one month. We shall return the good man to his home. We shall escort him into Rome; we shall earn the absolution. Then whoever wants to return can return, and whoever wants to stay can stay." This opinion won. The sixteen companies enlisted with Cola de Rienzi as his cavalrymen. He had some Perugians besides, sons of good men, and about a hundred Tuscan infantrymen as retainers. They wore cuirasses of the sort mercenaries wear. It was a noble and handsome brigade.

CHAPTER SIX

Public and solemn entrance of Cola into the city of Rome.

With these soldiers Cola came down through Tuscany; he passed valleys and mountains and dangerous places. He came as far as Orte without opposition. Then his arrival became known in Rome. The Romans joyfully prepared to welcome him; the aristocrats were on the alert, watching closely. He left Orte and went to Rome, in the year of our Lord thirteen fifty-three. The cavalry of Rome came all the way out to Monte Mario to meet him, with branches of olive in their hands as a sign of victory and peace. The people welcomed him joyfully, as if he were Scipio Africanus. Triumphal arches were built. He entered the Castel Sant'Angelo gate. Throughout the piazza of the Castel Sant'Angelo and the bridge, and the streets, arches made of bunting were hung, and ornaments of gold and silver. It seemed that all Rome could scarcely contain itself for joy. The happiness and good will of the people could not have been greater.

So he was honorably escorted up to the Palace of the Campidoglio, where he delivered a beautiful and eloquent speech. He said that for seven years he had been exiled from his home, as Nebuchadnezzar had been, but now, through the power of the virtuous God, he had returned to his senatorial seat by the voice of the Pope: not because he was worthy of such an office, but the Pope's voice had made him worthy. He added that he intended to raise up and reform the government of Rome. Then he made Messer Bettrone and Messer Arimbaldo de Narba Captains of War and gave them the banner of Rome; he made a certain Cecco de Peroscia, his councillor, a knight, and dressed him in gold.

The Romans held a great festival for him, as the Jews did for Christ, when He entered Jerusalem mounted on an ass. They honored Him, spreading carpets and olive branches before Him, singing: BENEDICTVS QVI VENIS. Finally they went home and left Him alone with His disciples in the piazza; there was no one who offered Him a little dinner.

The following day Cola de Rienzi met with some ambassadors from the surrounding area. Lord, how well he answered them! He gave replies; he made promises; he prepared himself to judge fervently.

CHAPTER SEVEN

Appearance and habits of Cola, who, after his arrival in Rome, demands the obedience of the barons. His orders are ignored and his messengers mistreated by Stefanello Colonna.

The barons were all watching carefully to see what would happen. His triumphal entry had drawn a large crowd. There were many banners; never was there so much pomp. There were infantrymen with swords on this side and that. It seemed clear that Cola wanted to rule by tyranny. Most of what he had lost had been returned to him. He sent edicts and letters through the towns and the district of Rome, describing his fortunate return. He wanted every man to prepare himself for the Good Estate.

Cola had changed his earlier habits drastically. He used to be sober, temperate, and abstinent; now he had become an intemperate drinker. He drank wine continually; at every hour he ate sweets and drank. He observed neither order nor time. He would mix Greek wine with Trebbian fiano, and malmsey with rebola. He was ready to drink at any hour. It was a horrible thing to see how much he would drink. He drank too much. He said that while in prison he had caught a quinsey. He had also become enormously fat. He had a round, triumphal belly, like an Asian abbot's. His skin shone like a peacock's; he was ruddy; he had a long beard. His expression would change suddenly, and his eyes become inflamed. His mind and his will would change like fire. He had clear eyes, but from time to time they would become as red as fire.

He had been in the summit of the Palace of the Campidoglio for four days when he summoned all the barons to come and pay him homage. Among the others he summoned Stefaniello della Colonna, who was in Palestrina. This Stefaniello had been a small boy at the time of the deaths of his father Stefano and his brother Janni Colonna, as was described earlier. Now he had retreated to the fort in Palestrina. To this Stefaniello Cola sent two Roman citizens, Buccio de Jubileo and Janni Cafariello, as ambassadors, instructing him to obey the commands of the holy Senate, under penalty of his wrath. Stefaniello seized these ambassadors and put one of them in a dark dungeon; he also drew out one of his teeth and fined him four hundred florins. The following day he overran the fields of Rome with his archers and brigands; he led off all the cattle. A clamor arose in Rome; mur-

murs about the looting the Romans had suffered reached the ears of the Tribune.

CHAPTER EIGHT

Cola, provoked by the disdain and the incursions of the Colonna, marches out against them and exhorts his forces to battle with a beautiful speech.

Then the Tribune rode out of the city with a few servants; he passed through the gate alone. The soldiers followed him, some armed, some not, as time permitted. They ran through the Porta Maggiore to the Via Praenestina, through wooded, deserted areas. The attempt was vain, useless. They found no one, neither the cattle nor the archers. The skilful archers and infantrymen of Palestrina had cleverly led off the loot and concealed it in a wood called Pantano, which lies between Tivoli and Palestrina. There they lay hidden. During the night they wisely took the loot out of Pantano and brought it to Palestrina.

After searching carefully and finding nothing, the Tribune's soldiers, since it was getting dark, went to the city of Tivoli, where they passed the night. Next morning came the news that the Romans' cattle had been taken out of Pantano and led to Palestrina. The Tribune was angry, and said, "What good does it do to wander here and there through trackless wastes? I will not fence with the house of Colonna any longer; I want to meet them face to face." He stayed in Tivoli four days. He sent out edicts. He ordered the Roman cavalry to come from Rome at once, with all the cavalrymen and troops of the infantry. He was a powerful writer. He set up his standard in Tivoli with his own arms of azure with a gold sun and silver stars, together with the arms of Rome. A strange thing happened: that standard did not shine as it did before; it stood there weak and flaccid; it did not wave proudly in the wind.

When his troop of soldiers had come, with many banners, bagpipes, and trumpets, and when Messer Bettrone and Messer Arimbaldo, whom he had named general Captain of War, had come, the soldiers complained that they wanted their pay. The German constables demanded money, claiming that they had been forced to pawn their arms. The Tribune found many excuses, but finally there was no longer any way out. Now see the filthy trick he played on his Captains. He met with Messer Bettrone and Messer Arimbaldo and said to them, "I find written in the Roman histories that once there was no money in the Commune of Rome for soldiers. The Consul gathered the barons and said to them, 'We who hold the offices and the dignities should be the first to give what we can, out of good will.' From this gift a great deal of money was collected, which was distributed to the militia. So you, too, ought to be the first to give. When the good people of Rome see that you foreigners are giving, they also will be prepared to give, and thus we shall have money to spare." The Captains then gave him a thousand florins, five hundred each, in two purses. The Tribune distributed this money among the mercenaries. To the infantry he gave half pay from money contributed by the people of Tivoli.

Then he assembled the people in the piazza of San Lorenzo of Tivoli and delivered a beautiful speech. He told them how he had gone wandering for seven years, and how he had come into favor with the Emperor Charles, whose aid he expected at any moment. He told them how he was in favor with the Pope, in spite of his enemies, the Colonna. Now he was Senator of Rome for the Pope, but he was not allowed to govern because of the tyranny of the Colonna, of that poisonous snake, that weed of the quagmires, Stefaniello della Colonna. Therefore he was determined to exterminate the house of Colonna, to lay them even lower than he had before. Theirs was an accursed house; because of their pride the city of Rome lived in poverty, while other countries lived in wealth. Then he added, "I have decided to move the army against Palestrina and devastate the entire area. Therefore I pray that you, the people of Tivoli, will accompany us with a good heart, and help us in our great need, and not abandon us."

CHAPTER NINE

Cola, strengthened with auxiliary forces, besieges Palestrina.

This speech was made from the parapet of the Palloni.[9] After these beautiful words were spoken, on the following day he moved his foreign infantry, his cavalry, and the people of Tivoli with supplies and baggage to battle, and mustered at Castiglione di Santa Prassede. He spent two days there; there the whole force gathered. Then he moved out on the following day, and attacked Palestrina with his whole force, in the year of our Lord thirteen fifty-three.[10] The Tribune besieged Palestrina and encamped his army at Santa Maria della Villa, two miles from the city. There were a thousand knights there, Romans and mercenaries; the people of Tivoli and Velletri were there, and the troops of the neighboring communes and of the Abbey of Farfa, and of Campagna and Montagna.

When the siege was set, no one did anything. Only he, Cola de Rienzi, kept his eyes continually on Palestrina. He raised his head and looked at the high hill, the strong castle, and considered how he could confound and ruin that edifice. Gazing constantly on the place, he said, "This is the mountain which I

9 A Tivoli family.
10 Again, the year should be 1354; the text adds here "month ***, day ***"; apparently the Chronicler was unable to ascertain the exact date of the battle.

must level." As he stared intently at Palestrina, he often saw cattle coming out through the upper gate to graze, and entering the upper gate to drink, and then returning to the pastures. He also saw men entering at the other upper gate with baggage trains loaded with supplies. He saw a long line of carts coming with provisions into Palestrina. Speaking to those who were with him, he asked, "Those baggage trains: what do they mean?" They answered, "Senator, those cattle are going out to pasture and returning to the water in Palestrina to drink; those men are carrying flour and supplies to feed the town and keep it from starving." He answered, "Tell me, wouldn't it be possible to capture the passes, to keep those cattle from going out to pasture so freely, and those men from carrying supplies?" The less loyal Romans answered, "The mountains of Palestrina are so rugged that those upper entrances and exits cannot be blocked off. The place is so savage that no army could stay there." But this was not true. The indolence of the Roman barons was another problem: they were waiting to see how it would all turn out; they refused to help.

Then the Tribune said, "I will never leave you until I destroy you, Palestrina. And if after the defeat of the Colonna at the gate of San Lorenzo I had ridden out with the people of Rome, I would have entered this town freely, without opposition. It would already be destroyed. I would not have endured this endless suffering; the people of Rome would be living in peace and rest."

CHAPTER TEN

The siege of Palestrina is lifted, and Cola, suspecting that Messer Morreale wishes to betray him, has him imprisoned.

On the second day after the army encamped, the pillaging was begun, and all the farm land of Palestrina was destroyed, the whole plain as far as the city. Nothing remained but the part above the town, less than a third. This little bit escaped destruction because after eight days the army left. There were two reasons for this departure. First, a quarrel had arisen between the people of Tivoli and those of Velletri, who suddenly deserted to Palestrina. It was therefore believed that further sedition was likely to arise within the army.

The second reason was that a maidservant of Messer Morreale, who had come to Rome to see his brothers, heard her master say many times that he wanted at any cost to kill Cola de Rienzi, who had stolen all their property; there was no hope of recovering it, and, what was worse, the Tribune was not even bothering to cajole them. What did the good woman do, I ask you? Because she had suffered many insults and outrages at the hands of her master, she went to find the Tribune, and, weeping, she revealed everything Messer Morreale had said he wanted to do. Therefore the Tribune summoned him at once, threw him in irons, and imprisoned him in the Campidoglio, along with his brothers, because they too had spoken ill of the Tribune and shared their brother's ill will toward him. Meanwhile the Tribune was searching for a way to destroy Palestrina, and was wondering where he could hunt up money to pay his soldiers, who were grumbling that they wanted their pay; and because of all this he was unhappy.

Now Fra Morreale, seeing that he had been caught by the work of his maidservant and realizing how much she could say, was very much afraid that she would be the ruin of him. However, he took heart. Knowing that the Tribune needed money, he decided to see if he could free himself in some way. He informed Messer Cola de Rienzi that if he let him go he would provide him with all the money and soldiers he needed and would give him everything he wanted.

And so Fra Morreale, thinking that he would be pardoned, said to his imprisoned brothers, Messer Arimbaldo and Messer Bettrone, "Let one or two of us stay here. Let me go. I'll bring him ten thousand, twenty thousand florins and as much money and as many men as he wants." His brothers answered, "Lord, do it, in God's name!" But Fra Morreale found no agent who could help him with this plan.

CHAPTER ELEVEN

Rigorous judgment and death of Messer Morreale.

When night came, Fra Morreale was awakened and led to torture. When he saw the cord,[11] he scorned it, saying contemptuously, "Didn't I say you were rustic villains? You want to put me to the torture: don't you see I'm a knight? How can you be so despicable?" However, he was hoisted a little. Then he said, "I was chief of the Great Company, and because I am a knight I wanted to live honorably. I took ransom from the cities of Tuscany; I taxed them; I robbed towns and captured the people." Then he was returned to where his brothers were.

Chained and placed in the stocks between his brothers, he realized that he was going to die. He asked for penance, and spent the whole night with a friar to whom he confessed himself and thus set his affairs in order. When he heard his brothers murmuring, he turned to them and spoke these words: "Sweet brothers, do not fear. You are young boys and have not yet experienced the waves of fortune; you will not die. I am dying and do not fear my death. My life was always full of tribulation. I

11 An instrument of torture; the victim's hands were bound behind his back and he was hoisted by the cord.

care nothing for living. I have never feared death. I am content to die in the city where the blessed Saints Peter and Paul died. Although our misadventure is your fault, Messer Arimbaldo, for leading me here into this labyrinth, I have no complaint about this. You will not die here. Don't feel sorry for me; I am dying willingly. I am a man; I was deceived like a bird; I was betrayed like other men. God will have pity on me. I was upright in this world; I will be upright before God. I am not afraid, because I came here with the intention of doing good. You are young: take care, for you have not known Fortune for what she is. I beg that you love one another and be valorous in the world as I was, who made myself master of Puglia, Tuscany, and the March." He kept repeating this until dawn appeared. He asked to hear Mass in the morning, and he heard it standing shoeless with naked legs.

At the hour of mid-tierce the bell was sounded and the people assembled. Fra Morreale was led up the stairway to the Lion, and stopped and knelt before the image of the Madonna. On his head he wore a dark hood decorated with gold. On his back he wore a jacket of brown velvet sewn with golden thread. He wore no belt; his stockings were dark; his hands were loosely bound; he held a cross in one hand. Three friars were with him.

When he heard the sentence, he said, "Ah, Romans, how can you consent to my death? I have never done you any wrong, but your poverty and my riches make me die." Then he said, "What have I come to? By my faith, I've had under my command ten times as many men as are here, and more." Then he said, "I am happy to die where Peter and Paul died. My life has not been without tribulation." Then he said, "Woe to that evil traitor after my death!" In the sentence the gallows was mentioned. At this he was deeply stunned, and stood as if dazed. Then those around him comforted him and calmed his fears;

they promised that he was condemned to be beheaded. At that he was content; he stood quietly.

He made his way to the esplanade; through the whole street he did not stop turning this way and that. He said, "Romans, I am dying unjustly. I am dying because of your poverty and my riches. I intended to set this city right." He kept speaking pitifully; pitifully he kissed the cross; he kept as tight a grip on himself as he could. A man of action, triumphant, a brilliant warrior: from the time of Caesar to the present day there has never been a better man. He was the man who arrived by chance; he was driven onto the Roman seashore during a storm, as was described above in the account of the beached galley.[12]

When he reached the esplanade, there where the foundations of the tower are, he circled the area, and knelt on the ground, and then got up, saying, "I have not placed myself properly." He turned toward the east and commended himself to God; then he knelt on the ground, kissed the block, and said, "God save thee, holy Justice." He made the sign of the cross over the block and kissed it; he drew off his hood and threw it away. When the axe was placed on his neck, he said, "I have not placed myself properly." There were many good people with him then, among whom was his surgeon. This man found the juncture. The iron was set; at the first blow his head leapt forward and fell. A few hairs from his beard remained on the block.

Some Minorites put his body in a casket. When his head was joined to his body it looked as if he had a ribbon of red silk around his neck. The excellent Fra Morreale, whose fame and glory resounded through all Italy, was entombed in Santa Maria d'Aracoeli. In the city of Tivoli there was a member of his household, a kinsman of his, who when he heard of the death of his lord died of uncontrollable sorrow the next day.

12 In Ch. 16 of the complete chronicle; Morreale was a passenger on the galley.

CHAPTER TWELVE

Cola announces his reasons for condemning Messer Morreale;
he names Riccardo degli Anniballi, Lord of Monte Compatri,
Captain of the People, and again besieges Palestrina and the
Colonna.

The Romans were deeply affected by the death of this valiant
man. Then the Tribune assembled the people and said, "Gentlemen, do not be disturbed at the death of this man, who was
the worst man in the world. He robbed cities and castles; he
killed and captured men and women; he took two thousand
women captive. And this time he came here to overthrow our
government, not to set it right. He planned to make himself absolute ruler of Rome; he planned to become master of the food
supply; he planned to devastate Campagna and the city of
Rome, and the rest of Italy as well. With God's help we shall
bring the war we are fighting to a happy conclusion, but for now
we shall do as a grain thresher does: throw the chaff and husks
to the wind and keep the grain for ourselves. So we have condemned this false man; his money, horses and arms we shall
take to conduct our war." These words calmed the Romans
somewhat.

Meanwhile an express letter came from the Legate ordering
Messer Arimbaldo to be sent to him safe and sound. This was
done. His brother, Messer Bettrone, remained in chains. The
Tribune took a large part of Fra Morreale's money. Not all of it,
because most of it had been taken by Messer Janni de Castiello,
whom the nobles of Rome looked upon as a traitor, because he
did not keep faith with his friend. Cola de Rienzi immediately
paid the soldiers, infantry and cavalry, who wished to remain.
The others he allowed to depart. He gathered a great number of
archers; he had about three hundred cavalrymen. He appointed

the wise and experienced warrior Liccardo Imprennente delli Anniballi, Lord of Monte Compatri, Captain of the People. He stationed his soldiers in the towns around Palestrina. He kept troops of infantry and archers in Frascati and a troop of infantry and archers in Colonna; he sent troops of infantry to Castiglione di Santa Prassede; the Marshall stayed in Tivoli.

The Tribune remained in Rome, in the Campidoglio, to make plans, to see what was to be done. He devoted a great deal of thought to finding money for the soldiers. He cut down his household expenses; he needed every penny for wages. Never was there seen such a man. He was the only one who thought of the Romans. He saw more standing in the Campidoglio than his officers did in the places where they were posted. He kept urging and writing to his officers. He showed them how to do things and how to get them done at once: how to blockade the passes through which attacks were being made, how to capture soldiers and spies. He never stopped.

But his officers were sluggish and cold; they did no notable deeds. Only the valiant warrior Liccardo did not hold back. He took loot night and day. He chased the Colonna through all Campagna; he did not let them rest; he wore out Stefaniello and the Colonna and the people of Palestrina. He was bringing the war to a good conclusion; he was a masterly man who knew the passes and the places and the times. He knew how to make the soldiers love him; they obeyed him willingly. The Hungarians would say, "Never was seen a captain so valorous." He would point and say, "Those cattle are coming here," and as he said it so they came. The war was turning out well.

CHAPTER THIRTEEN

Account of the unfortunate death of Cola.

Now I want to describe the death of the Tribune. The Tribune had levied a tax on wine and other commodities, which he called a "subsidy." It amounted to six pennies per load of wine. He collected a great deal of money. The Romans put up with it in order to have a government. To increase his revenues he also rationed salt, and lowered his personal and household expenses. His only thoughts were for his soldiers. Without warning he arrested a noble and worthy citizen of Rome, named Panalfuccio de Guido. He was a noble man, who wanted to be lord of the people; Cola cut off his head without pity or cause. At his death all Rome was disturbed.

The Romans were like quiet little sheep; they dared not speak; they feared the Tribune like a demon. When the council met he got everything he wanted; no councillor contradicted him. He would laugh and weep at the same instant, and pouring out tears and sighs he would laugh, so volatile and mobile was his will. Now he wept, now he caroused. Then he began arresting people; he arrested one man after another, and released them for ransom. The murmuring sounded quietly through Rome. Therefore to protect himself he enlisted fifty Roman infantrymen for each region of the city, ready at every alarm. He did not give them pay. He promised it. Every day he kept them in hire; he promised them a great deal of grain and other rewards. Finally, he dismissed Liccardo from his office and appointed new captains. This was his downfall. Liccardo ceased his looting and other military operations, grumbling, not unjustly, about Cola's ingratitude.

It was the month of September, the eighth day.[13] Cola de Rienzi was in bed that morning. He had washed his face. Suddenly from the northeast there came a voice crying, "Long live the people! Long live the people!" At this voice the people came through the streets from this side and that. The cry grew louder; more people gathered. At the market crossroads armed men gathered; they came from Sant'Angelo and from Ripa; they

13 The correct date is 8 October.

came from Colonna and from Trevi. When they had assembled, the cry was changed, and they said, "Death to the traitor Cola de Rienzi! Death!"

Now the young men crowded around in a rage, the very ones who were enlisted in the Tribune's militia. All of the regions of the city were not there, only those which have been named. They ran to the Palace of the Campidoglio. Then other people joined them, men and women and children. They threw rocks; they made noise and uproar; they surrounded the Palace on every side, in front and behind, saying, "Death to the traitor who made the tax! Death!" Their rage was terrible.

The Tribune made no defense against this; he did not sound the bell; he did not provide himself with men. And at first he said, "They say 'Long live the people,' and we say it too. It is to raise up the people that we are here; my soldiers are enlisted; the letter from the Pope confirming my position has arrived. All that remains is to announce it in the council." When he finally saw that the cry ended in evil, he was very frightened, especially because he had been deserted by every living person in the Campidoglio. Judges, notaries, servants, and everyone else had worked hard to save their skins. He was left alone with three people, among whom was Locciolo Pellicciaro, his kinsman. When the Tribune saw that the tumult of the people was growing and saw that he was deserted and defenseless, he was very frightened. He asked the three what was to be done.

Searching for a remedy, he gathered his courage and said, "I will not go thus, by my faith!" Then he armed himself completely in the style of a knight, and put the helmet on his head, his cuirass and falds and greaves. He took the banner of the people and stepped out onto the balcony of the upper hall alone. He stretched out his hand and signalled them to be quiet, since he wished to speak. Without doubt if they had listened to him he would have broken their wills and changed their minds and the plot would have failed. But the Romans refused to listen to him. They acted like pigs. They threw rocks; they shot missiles. They ran with torches to burn the gate. There were so many missiles and javelins that he could not stay on the balcony. A javelin struck his hand. Then he took the banner and stretched out the silk in both his hands; he showed the letters of gold, the arms of the citizens of Rome, as if to say, "You refuse to let me speak. Look! I am a citizen and plebeian like you; and if you kill me, you kill yourselves, who are Romans." But this was useless; it only made the mindless people worse. "Death to the traitor!" they shouted.

Unable to endure it any longer he looked for another way to save himself. He was afraid to stay in the upper hall, because this was where Messer Bettrone de Narba, to whom he had done such a great injury, was being held prisoner. He was afraid that he would kill him with his own hands. He knew and understood that Messer Bettrone was signalling to the people. He decided that it would be safer to leave the upper hall and get further away from Messer Bettrone. He took tablecloths from the table and tied them around his waist and lowered himself down into the courtyard in front of the prison. The prisoners were in the prison; they saw everything. He took the keys and kept them to himself. He was afraid of the prisoners.

Locciolo Pellicciaro remained in the upper hall; from time to time he appeared on the balcony and gestured and called to the people, saying, "There he is! He's coming down behind!" and they went behind the Palace, where he was coming. Then he went back to the Tribune, and encouraged him, telling him not to be afraid. Then he went back to the people and made similar signs: "He's there behind, he's there behind!" He gave them the way and the order. Locciolo killed him; Locciolo Pellicciaro destroyed the liberty of the people, who had never found a leader. Only with this man could they find liberty. If Locciolo had only encouraged him, he surely would not have died, because the hall was burnt, and the bridge of the stairway fell soon afterward; no one could have reached him. The day was getting on; the people of Regola and the other regions would have come; the crowd would have become larger and more diverse, and might have changed its mind. Everyone might have gone home, or indeed there might have been a great battle. But Locciolo took away his hope.

The Tribune in despair placed himself in the hands of fortune. Standing in the courtyard in front of the Cancellaria,[14] he took off his helmet and put it on again and again. This was because he had two different plans. The first plan was to die honorably, dressed in his armor, with his sword in his hand, like a magnificent and imperial person. And this he showed when he put on his helmet and took up his arms. The second plan was to save his life and not die. And this he showed when he took off his helmet. These two desires fought with each other in his mind. The winner was the desire to save himself and live. He was a man like any other; he was afraid to die.

Then he deliberated on the best possible way of keeping himself alive; he searched and found the way, a shameful and spiritless way. By this time the Romans had thrown fire on the first gate, wood, oil, and pitch. The gate was burning; the roof of the loggia was blazing; the second gate was burning and the roof and the timbers were falling piece by piece. The noise was horrible.

The Tribune decided to pass through the fire in disguise and mingle with the others and save his life. This was his final plan. He found no other way. And so he stripped off his noble insignia; he threw away all his armor. It is a sorrowful thing to

14 Part of the Palace of the Campidoglio; a prison and salt storeroom built into the ruins of the Tabularium.

relate! He snipped off his beard and tinted his face with black coloring. Nearby there was a little lodge where the porter slept. He went in there and took an old cloak of vile cloth, of the sort shepherds wear in the Campagna. He dressed himself in this vile cloak; then he put a coverlet from the bed over his head and thus disguised he went down. He passed the gate, which was burning; he passed the stairway and the roof tower, which was falling; he passed the last gate freely. The fire did not touch him; he mingled with the others in his changed form. He changed his accent and spoke like a peasant and said, "Up, up to the traitor!"

If he passed the last stairway he was free; the people had their minds on the Palace. He passed the last gate. A man appeared before him and recognized him. He held up his hand and said, "Wait a minute. Where're you going?" He took the feather-bolster from his head, but what gave the Tribune away most of all was the splendor of the bracelets he wore. They were gold; they did not look like cheap stuff. Then, since he was discovered, the Tribune revealed himself completely; he showed who he was. He could no longer escape. There was no remedy but standing to mercy, to the will of others. He was taken by the arms and led without resistance through all the stairways as far as the place of the Lion, where others had heard their sentences, where he had passed sentence on others. There he was led; a silence fell. No man was bold enough to touch him. There he stood for almost an hour, his beard cut, his face black as a baker's, in a loose jacket of green silk, with gold trimmings, with blue stockings like those barons wear. His arms were folded. In the silence he moved his face; he looked this way and that. Then Cecco dello Viecchio took a dagger in his hand and stabbed him in the stomach.

He was the first. Immediately afterward Laurentio de Treio, the notary, struck his head with a sword. Then one man after another stabbed him; one struck, another swore to. He made no sound; he died at once; he felt no pain. A man came with a rope and tied his feet together. They threw him on the ground, dragging him and peeling off his skin; they pierced him until he looked like a sieve. Everyone joked about it; they seemed to be at a festival. In this way he was dragged as far as San Marcello. There he was hung from a balcony by the feet: he had no head. The bones of his skull were left behind on the road where he had been dragged. He had so many wounds that he looked like a sieve. There was no place without a wound. His fat guts dangled from his belly. He was horribly fat. He was white as bloody milk. He was so fat that he looked like a giant buffalo or cow in a slaughterhouse. He hung there two days and one night. The boys threw rocks at him. On the third day, at the command of Jugurta and Sciarretta della Colonna, he was dragged to the Campo dell'Austa.

There all the Jews were gathered, a great multitude; not one was left behind. There a fire of dry thistles was made; he was put in this fire of thistles. He was fat; because he was so fat he burnt easily and freely. The Jews were very busy there, hurrying, crowded; they stirred the thistles to make them burn. Thus the corpse was burnt and reduced to powder; not a speck was left. Such was the end of Cola de Rienzi, who made himself Tribune August of Rome, who wanted to be champion of the Romans.

In his room was found a mirror of highly polished steel, covered with characters and figures. He had used this mirror to control the spirit of Fiorone.[15] Tablets also were found, in which he had written down the names of the Romans, and the levy which he had planned to make. The first order was of one hun-

15 It was on such evidence that Cola was accused of witchcraft by his enemies after his death; this would be the Colonna's excuse for forcing the Jews to destroy his body.

dred persons at five hundred florins; the second order, one hundred persons at four hundred florins; the third, one hundred florins; the fourth, fifty florins; and the fifth, ten florins. When this man was killed it was the year of our Lord thirteen fifty-three on the eighth day of September at the hour of tierce.[16] His death was not the only result of the people's rage: his mercenaries were robbed of all their equipment; they lost their horses and arms. Both those who were found in Rome and those who were stationed in the fortresses outside the city were left naked.

I want to enlarge a little on this material. In the time of Camillus the French entered Rome and beseiged Tarpeia, the Campidoglio hill.[17] The Romans had retreated there for fear. When they saw that there was not enough food in Tarpeia, they deliberated as to whether they should send the old men out, since they were useless, in order to save their food for the young men. This was done. The old men held a council before leaving Tarpeia; they said this: "We are going out to our houses among the French to be butchered; we shall die without doubt. It is better that we die in the clothing of virtue than of misery. Let each man put on his decorations." This was done. The old men went out to their houses; each one decorated himself in his official ornaments. Some dressed themselves in the clothing of a pontifex, some in that of a senator, some of a consul. They seated themselves on their decorated thrones, with their scepters, adorned with precious stones and gold, in their hands. Among the others was one named Papirius. Bravely adorned he stood in front of his house, wearing his senatorial toga and robe of state. In the morning the French wondered at such a strange thing; they ran

16 Actually 8 October 1354.
17 This incident, described in Livy 5.41, took place, according to tradition, in 390 B.C. The "French" are of course the Gauls.

in amazement to see it. A Frenchman took the beard of this Papirius and said, "Ah, old man, old man!" Papirius was outraged because the Frenchman did not speak to him with the reverence his dress demanded; he stretched out his staff and struck the Frenchman on the head; he did not fear to die to preserve his honor and majesty. This good Roman, then, refused to die with a coverlet on his head, the way Cola de Rienzi died.

SELECT BIBLIOGRAPHY

Barzini, L., "Cola di Rienzo or the Obsession of Antiquity," in *The Italians* (New York 1964) 117-132.

Bertoni, G., "La lingua della 'Vita di Cola di Rienzo,'" in *Lingua e pensiero* (Florence 1932) 73-84.

Bulwer-Lytton, E., *Rienzi: The Last of the Roman Tribunes* (London 1835).

Burdach, K., and P. Piur, *Briefwechsel des Cola di Rienzo* (Berlin 1912-29).

Castellani, G., "I 'Fragmenta Romanae Historiae': Studio preparatorio alla nuova edizione di essi," *Archivio della R. Società romana di Storia patria* 43 (1920) 113-156, 411-427; 44 (1921) 37-59.

Cecchelli, C., "Roma mediœvale," in *Topografia e urbanistica di Roma* (*Storia di Roma* XXII; Bologna 1958) 187-341.

Contini, G., "Invito a un capolavoro," *Letteratura* 4 (1940) 3-6.

Cosenza, M. E., *Francesco Petrarca and the Revolution of Cola di Rienzo* (Chicago 1913).

Cusin, F., ed., *Vita di Cola di Rienzo* (Florence 1943).

D'Annunzio, G., *Vite di uomini illustri e di uomini oscuri: La vita di Cola di Rienzo* (Milan 1913).

Davis, C. T., *Dante and the Idea of Rome* (Oxford 1957).

Douie, D. L., *The Nature and the Effect of the Heresy of the Fraticelli* (Manchester 1932).

Duprè Theseider, E., *Roma dal commune di popolo alla signoria pontificia* (*Storia di Roma* XI; Bologna 1952).

Ferguson, W. K., *The Renaissance in Historical Thought* (Cambridge, Mass. 1948).

Fleischer, V., *Rienzo: The Rise and Fall of a Dictator* (Port Washington, N. Y. 1970²).

Frugoni, A., ed., *Vita di Cola di Rienzo* (Florence 1957).

Gabrielli, A., ed., *Epistolario di Cola di Rienzo* (Rome 1890; repr. Turin 1966).

Ghisalberti, A. M., ed., *La vita di Cola di Rienzo* (Rome 1928).

Gibbon, E., "Restoration of the Freedom and Government of Rome by the Tribune Rienzi; His Virtues and Vices, his Expulsion and Death," in Ch. 70 of *The History of the Decline and Fall of the Roman Empire*, ed. J. B. Bury (London n.d.) VII 259-280.

Graf, A., *Roma nella memoria e nelle immaginazioni del medio evo* (Turin 1915²).

Gregorovius, F., *History of the City of Rome in the Middle Ages*, tr. A. Hamilton (London 1894-1902).

Mollat, G., *The Popes at Avignon: 1305-1378*, tr. J. Love (London 1963). (For bibliography see the latest French ed., *Les Papes d'Avignon* [Paris 1964¹⁰]).

Morghen, R., *Cola di Rienzo Senatore*, ed. L. Gatto (Rome 1956).

——, *I. La formazione della storiografia sul medioevo; II. Cola di Rienzo Tribuno*, ed. L. Gatto (Rome [1955]).

Muratori, L. A., ed., *Historiae romanae fragmenta*, tr. P. H. Gherardi, in *Antiquitates italicae medii aevi* (Milan 1740; repr. Bologna 1965) III 247-548.

Olschki, C., "Note bibliografiche su la Vita di Cola di Rienzo dell' Anonimo," *Roma* 2 (1924) 115-118.

Papencordt, F., *Cola di Rienzo und seine Zeit* (Hamburg 1841).

Partner, P., *The Lands of St. Peter: The Papal State in the Middle Ages and the Early Renaissance* (Berkeley 1972).

Pietrangeli, C., "Il palazzo Senatorio nel Medioevo," *Capitolium* 35.1 (1960) 3-19.

Pirodda, G., "Per una lettura della *Cronica* di Dino Compagni," *Filologia e letteratura* 13 (1967) 337-393.

Piur, P., *Cola di Rienzo: Darstellung seines Lebens und seines Geistes* (Vienna 1931).

Reeves, M., *The Influence of Prophecy in the Later Middle Ages: A Study in Joachimism* (Oxford 1969).

Ugolini, F. A., "La prosa degli 'Historiae romanae fragmenta' e della cosidetta 'Vita di Cola di Rienzo,'" *Archivio della R. Deputazione romana di Storia patria* 58 (1935) 1-68.

——, "Preliminari al testo critico degli *Historiae romanae fragmenta*," *Archivio della Deputazione romana di Storia patria* 68 (1945) 63-74.

Wagner, R., *Rienzi: der letzte der Tribunen,* in *Dramatische Werke* I, ed. K. Reuschel (Leipzig 1918) 41-107.

Waley, D., *The Italian City-Republics* (London 1969).

Weiss, R., *The Renaissance Discovery of Classical Antiquity* (Oxford 1969).

Wilkins, E. H., *Life of Petrarch* (Chicago 1961).

——, *Studies in the Life and Works of Petrarch* (Cambridge, Mass. 1955).

INDEX

Note: Members of the baronial clans of the Colonna and the Orsini are listed under these two family names; members of Cola ri Rienzo's family are listed under his name; other fourteenth-century Italians are listed under their own first names, with cross-references included when these seemed necessary. Readers wishing further information about the persons listed should begin by checking the index to Gregorovius (see bibliography). Geographical terms (such as the names of cities in Italy) are listed individually; they have all been modernized and thus can be found in atlases and gazetteers. Topographical details of the city of Rome are listed under "Rome"; since with only a few exceptions (all mentioned in the notes) Roman topographical nomenclature has been preserved to our own time, the churches, palaces, etc., listed here can be found in any good modern guidebook to Rome.

Acquapendente, 109

Acuto, Fra, 57-61

Agnilo de Montecielo, Fra, Joachite prophet, 20, 126

Agnilo Malabranca della Pescina, Chancellor of Rome, 66, 82

Albornoz, Gil d': see Egidio Conchese

allegory, use of, 19, 33-35, 36, 37-38, 125

Altamura (Puglia), 94

Amelia, 64, 109, 111

Ancona, 111, 113, 115, 120

Andrew, King of Puglia, 65, 69, 94

Aniballo de Ceccano, Cardinal Legate, 25, 48, 97-103, 128 ; his nephew, Janni, 103

Antiochia, 55

anticlericalism, 19, 114, 120-121

Aquileia, 59

Arezzo, 64, 130

Arimbaldo de Narba, Provençal adventurer, 17, 130-133, 135, 138, 141-143, 145

Aristotle, 60-62

Assisi, 64

Avignon, 14, 31, 48, 64, 77, 93, 99, 100, 110, 127-128

Babylon, 33, 50

Bari, 92, 94

Barzini, L., 16, 155

Becker, M., 12

Benedict XII, Pope, 36n.

Bertinoro, 114, 120

Bertoni, G., 20n., 155

Bertonuccio, plebeian of Cesena, 116, 117

Bertrand de Déaux, Cardinal Legate, 79-80, 91, 93, 128

Bettrannio dallo Poijetto, Cardinal of Ostia, 114

Bettrone de Narba, Provençal adventurer, 130, 131, 133, 135, 138, 141-143, 145, 149
Bible, exempla from, 17, 67-68, 135 ; quotations from, 13, 22, 66, 67, 103n., 125 n.
Boniface VIII, Pope, 15, 81
Bologna, 21, 65
Bolsena, 109
Bracciano, 20
Buccio de Jubileo, Cola's swordbearer and ambassador, 52, 136
Bulwer-Lytton, E., 16n., 155
Byron, Lord, 16n.

Canino, 109, 110
Cannae, Battle of, 88n., 89
Capranica, Castle of, 69
Carthage, 33, 88
Cassius Parmensis, 60
Castellani, G., 20n., 155
Castelluza (Marino), 79
Castiglione di Santa Prassede (Palestrina), 139, 146
Castile, King of, 109
Castrocaro, 114
Cavicchia, A., 12
Cecchelli, C., 155
Ceccano, 101
Cecco d'Alesso, Cola's standardbearer, 52
Cecco de Peroscia, Cola's councillor, 135
Cecco dello Viecchio, Cola's assassin, 151
Cecco Mancino, Cola's Chancellor, 93
ceremonies, descriptions of, 51-53, 69-74, 90, 134-135
Ceri, Castle of 62

Cesena, 114, 115, 116-119
Charles IV, Holy Roman Emperor, 17, 93, 112, 125-127, 138
Cicero, 16, 31
Città di Castello, 68
Civitavecchia, 62, 93, 110
classical antiquity, exempla from, 21, 24, 27, 59, 60, 88-90, 108, 134, 138, 153-154.
classical literature : see Aristotle, Cicero, Livy, Lucan, Sallust, Seneca, Valerius Maximus
Clement V, Pope, 14
Clement VI, Pope, 17, 29, 31, 32, 32n., 47, 64, 66, 72, 97, 109
clothing, descriptions of, 36, 45, 49, 51, 52, 65, 68, 71, 74, 75, 77, 80, 132, 133, 143, 151, 153
Cola de Buccio de Braccia (Vraccia), Roman baron, 62, 83
Cola di Rienzo : for major events in his career see Table of Contents ; his name, 15 ; his family : mother, Matalena, 31 ; father, Rienzi, 31 ; uncle, Janni Varvieri, 63 ; brother, 31 ; sister, 63 ; wife, 63, 70, 74, 93 ; mother-in-law, 70 ; son, Lorienzo, 81, 90 ; kinsman and betrayer, Locciolo Pellicciaro, 148-150
Cola Farfaro, Roman baron, 88
Cola Guallato, Cola's standardbearer, 41
Cola Pali de Molara, Roman baron, 88
Colonna (town), 146
Colonna : Andreuozzo de Normanno, 32, 33 ; Janni della Colonna, Cardinal, 32, 48 ; Jugurta della Colonna, 152 ;

Pietro de Agabito (Agapito) della Colonna, 54, 75, 83, 86-88 ; Sciarra della Colonna, 14, 81n., 91 ; Sciaretta della Colonna, 83, 152 ; Stefano della Colonna the Elder, 40, 43-44, 45, 54, 74-76 ; Stefano della Colonna (Stefano the Elder's son), 35, 44, 45, 56, 75, 81, 83, 85-88, 136 ; Janni Colonna (Stefano the Elder's grandson), 35, 37, 44, 62, 75, 83-88, 136 ; Stefaniello della Colonna (Stefano the Elder's grandson), 136, 138, 146

Compagni, D., 23

Constantine, Roman Emperor, 71, 73

Constantinople, 59

Conte, son (or nephew) of Cecco Mancino, member of Cola's government, 41, 93

Contini, G., 20n., 155

Corneto (now Tarquinia), 40, 43, 56, 70, 110

Cortona, 130n.

Cosenza, M. E., 16n., 155

crusades, 14, 115, 120-121

Cusin, F., 155

D'Annunzio, G., 155

Dante, 13, 14, 49n.

Davis, C. T., 16n., 155

De Carrara, Signori of Padua, 65

Dionysius of Syracuse, 24, 108

Douie, D. L., 20n., 155

Duprè Theseider, E., 13n., 16, 155

Durazzo, Duke of, 65

Egidio Conchese (Don Gilio, Gil d'Albornoz), Cardinal Legate, 24, 109-120, 128, 129, 133

Esmeduccio de Santo Severino, Corporal of the March, 112

excommunications, 93, 101, 108, 114, 128

executions, 49-50, 69, 142-144

Faenza, 120

Fano, 113

Fei, Andrea, 20

Ferguson, W. K., 155

Ferrara, 63

Ferrara, Marquises of, 47

Filino, 130

Filippino da Gonzaga, Tyrant of Mantua, 65

Fleischer, V., 16n., 155

Florence, 64, 110, 112, 130

Fonneruglia de Treio, Roman plebeian, 85

food and wine, lists and descriptions of, 53, 70, 73, 74, 102, 136

Forlì, 65, 114, 115, 120

Forlimpopolo, 114

Fossombrone, 113

Francesco delli Ordelaffi, Captain of Forlì, 65, 113-131 ; his wife, Cia, 116-119 ; his son, Janni 115, 119, 120 ; his son, Lodovico, 115-116 ; his daughter, 120

Francesco de Saviello, Roman baron, 45

Frascati, 146

Fraticelli : see Joachimism

Frugoni, A., 20n., 28, 155

Fuligno, 64

Gabrielli, A., 32n., 155

Gaeta, 65

Gaetani : see Boniface VIII, Jacovo, Janni

162 INDEX

Garibaldi, G., 15, 16n.
Gentile da Magliano, Corporal of the
  March, 111
Ghisalberti, A. M., 20n., 28, 155
Giaggiolo, 114
Gibbon, E., 156
Gil d'Albornoz: see Egidio Con-
  chese
Giorgio delli Tumberti of Cesena,
  117, 118
Giovanni: see Janni
Graf, A., 156
Gregorovius, F., 13n., 16n., 156
Gregory the Great, Pope, 58
Guido da Prato, physician, 102
guilds, 68

Hamilton, A., 156
Hannibal, 88-90
Henry VII, Holy Roman Emperor,
  14, 15, 126
heraldry (banners, coats of arms,
  etc.), 41, 46, 48, 52, 54, 71, 76,
  137, 149
heresy: see excommunications, patarine
Hungary, 65

Imola, 114
Innocent VI, Pope, 23, 107, 109,
  128
inscriptions, ancient, 17, 35-36
Isidore, St., 21, 23
Italian literature: see Compagni,
  Dante, Petrarch, Villani
Italy, union of, 18-19

Jacovo delli Vastardi, plebeian of
  Cesena, 116, 117
Jacovo Gaetano, Cardinal, 49
Janni, Court of Valmontone, 110

Janni Cafariello, Cola's ambassador,
  136
Janni de Allo, Cola's cupbearer, 51-
  52
Janni de Castiello, Roman baron,
  145
Janni de Lucca, Fra, Commander of
  the Holy Ghost, 98-99
Janni de Vico, Tyrant of Viterbo, 20,
  55-57, 62, 82, 91, 109-111; his
  son, Francesco, 62, 82, 91
Janni Gaetano, Count of Fondi, 62
Janni Pipino, Paladin of Altamura,
  92, 94, 102n.
Janni Visconte, Archbishop of
  Milan, 97
Janni Zaganella, plebeian of Cesena,
  116, 117
Jerusalem, 33, 135
Jews, 63, 67, 92, 135, 152
Joachimism, 19-20, 126
Joan, Queen of Puglia, 66, 69
John, King of France, 121n.
John XXII, Pope, 14
Jordano delli Aretini, Roman baron,
  88
Jubilee of 1350, 32n., 36-37, 95-
  103
Julius Caesar, 17, 31, 60
Jumentaro dalla Pira, Corporal of the
  March, 112

Laurentio de Treio, Cola's assassin,
  151
Leo I, Pope, 59
Lex regia of Vespasian, 35-36
Liccardo Imprennente delli Anniballi,
  Captain of the People of Rome,
  146, 147
Liello Migliaro, member of Cola's
  government, 52

Livy, 16, 17, 21, 22, 23, 28, 31, 88-90, 131, 153n.
Lomo da Esci, Corporal of the March, 112
Louis, King of Hungary, 65, 67, 69, 130
Louis, Prince of Taranto, 65, 66
Louis of Bavaria, Holy Roman Emperor, 14, 47, 65, 72
Love, J., 156
Luca de Saviello, Roman baron, 75, 91
Lucan, 21
Luchino (Lucchino), Tyrant of Milan, 47, 65

Macchantrevola (Marino), 79
Macerata, 113
Maiella, 125
Malabranca : see Agnilo, Mattheo
Malatesta of Rimini, 65, 111, 113, 115, 116, 118 ; his brother, Galiotto, 111-113, 115, 116, 118
Manfredi, noblemen of Romagna, 120
Mantua, 65
Marcian, Roman Emperor, 59, 62
Marcus Aurelius, Roman Emperor, 73n
Marino, 77-80, 86, 90
Mark Antony, 60
Marseilles, 49n.
Marta, 109, 110
Martino de Puorto, Roman baron, 48-50, 51 ; his wife, Mascia delli Alberteschi, 49
Martinus Polonus, Fra, 59
Mastino della Scala, Tyrant of Verona, 63
Mattheo, son of Agnilo Malabranca, Roman baron, 82

Mattheo da Viterbo, physician, 102
mediaeval Latin literature : see Gregory the Great, Isidore, Joachimism, Martinus Polonus
medicine and physiology, 49, 58, 60-62, 102, 103, 136
Merulus, Fra, 58-59
Milan, 97, 98n.
military operations, descriptions of, 56, 77-79, 84, 115, 118-119, 120, 139-140
Minervino, 92, 94
Molieti, 64
Mollat, G., 13n., 156
Monte Cassino, 89, 102
Monte Feltrano, 130
Monte Mario, 134
Montefiascone, 109, 128, 129
Monticelli (Tivoli), 62
Morghen, R., 13n., 16n., 156
Morreale, Fra, Provençal adventurer, 24, 25, 130, 131-132, 141-144, 145
Muratori, L. A., 102n., 156
music and musical instruments, 48, 52-53, 70, 73, 76, 81, 84-87, 113
Muslims, 50-51, 109n.

Naples, Princes of, 47, 50, 92, 94
Narbonne, 130
Narni, 56, 109, 111
Nepi, 78
Nicola da Buscareto, follower of Egidio Conchese, 112

Obizzo, Marquis of Ferrara, 65
Octavian, 21, 60
Olschki, C., 156
Orsini (Orzini) : Cola Orsino (Urzino), 55, 75, 82 ; Jordano de Marini, 56, 75, 75-79, 83, 86,

91 ; Jordano delli Orzini dello Monte, 45, 56, 75, 82, 110 ; Orzo de Vicovaro delli Orzini, 75 ; Ranallo delli Orsini de Marini, 45, 75, 76, 77-79 ; Rinaldo Orsini, papal notary, 77n. ; Vertuolla delli Orzini, 23, 69, 75, 107-108 ; his son, Lubertiello, 75, 82
Orte, 134
Orvieto, 89, 109, 110, 111
Ostia, 114
Otto III, Holy Roman Emperor, 14

Padua, 65
paintings, 19, 33-35, 37-38, 78, 93
Palazzino, plebeian of Cesena, 116, 117
Palestrina, 44, 81, 136, 137, 139, 140, 141, 146
Panalfuccio de Guido, Roman baron, 147
Pannolfo of the Lords of Belvedere, Roman baron, 86
Pantano (Palestrina), 137
Papencordt, F., 156
Papirius, 153-154
Partner, P., 156
patarine (epithet for heretic), 98, 98n., 101, 120, 127
Paterno (Ancona), 113
Pavia, 88
Pavolo Buffa, soldier in Cola's army, 83
Peraham, Sultan of Babylon, 50-51
Perugia, 56, 63, 70, 109, 110, 112, 129-131
Perugia, Lake of, 88
Pesaro, 113
Petrarch, 13, 17, 32n., 36n.
Philip of Valois, King of France, 66
Pietrangeli, C., 156

Piglio, 62
Pirodda, G., 20n., 156
Pistoia, 64
Piur, P., 155, 156
Polo de Libano, Roman baron, 88
Ponceletto della Cammora, Senate scribe, 53
Porto, Castle of, 49, 62
Prague, 93, 126-127
prodigies, miracles, dreams, etc., 23n., 47, 57-62, 71, 81, 83
Provence, 120, 130

Raimond de Chameyrac, Bishop of Orvieto, papal vicar, 41, 43, 44, 64, 71, 73, 74
Ranieri de Busa, 110
Recanati, 111
Redolfo de Camerino, Corporal of the March, 112
Reeves, M., 16n., 156
revolutions, coups, popular uprisings, etc. : in Rome, 40-44, 92-93, 98-99, 107-108, 147-152 ; in Cesena, 117-118
Riccardo : see Liccardo
Rieti, 62, 64
Rimini, 65, 113, 116
Rispampani, 55, 57, 110
Rome : general description, 44 ; ancient monuments : basin of Constantine, 71 ; "Horse of Constantine" (i.e., equestrian statue of Marcus Aurelius), 73 ; Lion of the Campidoglio, 49, 143, 151 ; Pantheon, 47n., 57 ; Tabularium, 150n. ; Aventine Hill, 39 ; bridges : bridge of the Castel Sant'-Angelo, 134 ; bridge of St. Peter, 52, 80 ; Ponte della Paglia, 39 ; Ponte di Ceperano, 39 ; Ponte

Molle, 57 ; *churches and basilicas* : Sant'Angelo delle Scale, 100 ; Sant'Angelo in Pescheria, 37-38, 40, 92 ; San Celso, 80 ; San Crisogono, 101 ; San Giorgio in Velabro, 38 ; St. John Lateran, 35-37, 51, 70, 71, 72 ; San Lorenzo fuori le Mura, 44, 82 ; San Lorenzo in Piscibus, 99-101 ; San Marcello, 28, 43, 152 ; Santa Maria d'Aracoeli, 87, 144 ; Santa Maria Maddalena, 125 ; Santa Maria Rotunda, 57 ; St. Paul's, 99 ; St. Peter's, 51-53, 63, 80, 98n., 99, 103 ; San Salvatore in Pesoli, 92 ; San Silvestro in Capite, 88 ; Santo Spirito, 99, 103 ; San Tommaso, 31 ; *gates* : Castel Sant'Angelo gate, 134 ; Porta Maggiore, 137 ; Porta San Giovanni, 78 ; Porta San Lorenzo (Porta Tiburtina), 25, 82-87, 140 ; *palaces* : Campidoglio, 25-27, 33, 41, 44, 45, 46, 49, 53-54, 56, 63, 75, 78, 89, 91, 107-108, 135, 136, 141-144, 146, 148-151, 153 ; Castel Sant'Angelo, 55, 66, 82, 93, 125, 134 ; Colonna Palace, 28 ; Lalli Palace, 93 ; Lateran Palace, 70-74 ; Orsini palaces, 84 ; Papal Palace (Vatican), 97, 98, 100 ; *piazzas* : Campo de' Fiori, 68 ; Piazza di San Marcello, 43 ; piazza of the Castel Sant'Angelo, 125, 134 ; Portico of the Armenians, 99 ; *regions* : Camigliano, 47 ; Colonna, 148 ; Portica, 98 ; Regola, 31, 51, 150 ; Ripa, 147 ; Sant'-Angelo, 147 ; Trevi, 148 ; Temple of the Jews, 31

Robert, King of Naples, 14, 94

Sagunza (Spain), 88
Sallust, 21
San Germano, 102
San Giorgio, Villa of, 103-104
Savelli : *see* Francesco, Luca
Savignano, 117
Savoy, Count of, 115, 120
Scaraglino, nobleman of Cesena, 117, 118
Scarpetta, Constable in Cola's army, 92
Seneca, 16, 31
Siena, 64, 110, 130
Spoleto, 64, 88
Stefaniello, called Magnacuccia, notary, 41
Sylvester I, Pope, 71

Taddeo delli Pepoli, Tyrant of Bologna, 65
Taranto, 65
Tarifa (Spain), 109
taxes, 18, 28, 39, 55, 91, 146-147, 152-153
Terni, 64, 109
Tiber (river), 62, 78
Tiberius, Roman Emperor, 36
Ticino (river), 88
Tivoli, 62, 64, 121, 137, 138, 139, 144, 146
Todi, 56, 64
Todino de Antonio, 64
Tomao de Fortifiocca, Senate scribe, 33, 53
Tortora, a courier, 50
Toscanella, 128-129
Trasimene, Lake, Battle of, 88n., 89
Troy, 33

Ugolini, F. A., 20n., 28, 156

Valerius Maximus, 16, 31, 60, 108

166 INDEX

Velletri, 64, 141
Venice, 65
Venice, Doge of, 47
Verona, 65
Vespasian, Roman Emperor, 35, 36
Vetralla, 56, 58
Via Praenestina, 137
Vico Scuotto, Roman knight, 71-72
Villani, G., 16n., 23
Visconte : see Janni

Viterbo, 55, 56, 62, 103, 109, 110, 111, 129
Vitorchiano, 52, 62
Volturno (river), 89

Wagner, R., 16n., 158
Waley, D., 16n., 158
Weiss, R., 16n., 158
Wilkins, E. H., 158